For Sall.

Rememb

Lots of love from
Sam's Mum!

Fiona x

+ Jim Peters

FOLK TALES
OF THE
EVER AFTER
STORIES ABOUT DEATH,
DYING AND BEYOND

FIONA COLLINS AND JUNE PETERS

FOLK TALES
OF THE
EVER AFTER
STORIES ABOUT DEATH,
DYING AND BEYOND

ILLUSTRATED BY JUNE PETERS

The
History
Press

In Memory of Ed and Robbie

First published 2023

The History Press
97 St George's Place, Cheltenham,
Gloucestershire, GL50 3QB
www.thehistorypress.co.uk

British Library Cataloguing in Publication Data.
A catalogue record for this book is available from the British Library.

ISBN 978 0 75099 890 1

Typesetting and origination by The History Press
Printed and bound in Great Britain by TJ Books Limited, Padstow, Cornwall.

Trees for LYfe

Contents

FOREWORD

By Alida Gersie

This is an intimate book. Oral storytelling is, of course, an ancient and intimate human tradition. However, the words 'death and intimacy' are less frequently uttered in one breath. And when they are, it is primarily to convey a sense of brokenness or rupture. Grief wounds us so. The death of people, pets and other beings hurts.

So, how can a collection of finely retold traditional stories about dying and death be intimate? The book generates intimacy mostly through the authors' choice of stories. Taken together, this is an intriguing, occasionally defiant, and at times, a witty bunch of tales. Quite a few stories will be comfortably familiar, yet fresh in their retelling. Others are new gems. A warm quality is also generated through the stories' arrangement in carefully thought through sections. Each section has a stirring personal introduction in which the authors' creative humanity shines through.

The presence of birth, growth and death in our life is ubiquitous and irrevocable. Our own death is inevitable. This remarkable collection enables us to embrace the life that is ours to live that bit more humanely.

It is a bighearted gift.

Alida Gersie PhD, Enfield, August 2022
Writer, story-gatherer and consultant in personal change

INTRODUCTION

BY FIONA

The idea for a book of folk tales about death and dying was born when my partner Ed died, after a long illness, in January 2020. Ed and I had worked together on five books for The History Press, with me choosing the words and Ed creating images. This is the first book I've written that he hasn't illustrated, and I was really glad when my closest friend June said she would work on it with me, contributing both images and stories.

My interest in death, and how humans think and feel about it, had already been fostered by taking part in Dying Matters Week events over some years, and by attending and hosting Death Cafés.

The traumatic death of my mother in 1990 had a long and profound effect on me. Family, friends and professionals were at a loss as to how to comfort me, until the wise storyteller Mary Medlicott suggested I read Alida Gersie's book on bereavement, *Storymaking in Bereavement: Dragons Fight in the Meadow*.

Alongside her advice on the processes of grieving, and how to live with and through them, Alida's book includes summaries of folk tales, myths and legends from around the world, exploring death, dying and grief. In all this treasure store, there was one image that really spoke to me: Inanna in the Underworld, hanging 'like a corpse' from a hook on the wall. This was exactly how I felt then: numbed, helpless, hopeless and cut off from life.

Reading Alida's book created a connection between me and that story that has nurtured me for more than thirty years. Inanna had to be in this book. If you want to know more about the story, the goddess and the culture from which she comes, look for Diane Wolkstein's book, co-written with the scholar, Samuel Noah Kramer.

Folk tales are made for retelling, and in the retelling, we all have the opportunity to use the tale to explore our beliefs and views and create new beliefs and new views. June and I have worked as professional storytellers in many settings for thirty years. We have chosen the stories for this book, both from our own repertoires and from the stories that other storytellers have offered us. We are telling these stories here, in our own words and in our own ways.

Our narratives contain fragments of folk wisdom, foolishness, belief, knowledge and jokes about death that have been passed on, first orally, then in written forms, around the world. Now we two tell them. When you've read them, you can tell them too.

References in this Introduction:

Alida Gersie, *Storymaking in Bereavement: Dragons Fight in the Meadow* (London: Jessica Kingsley, 1991).

Diane Wolkstein & Samuel Noah Kramer, *Inanna: Queen of Heaven and Earth* (New York: Harper & Row, 1983).

Dying Matters Week – www.hospiceuk.org/our-campaigns/
    dying-matters
Death Cafés – deathcafe.com

If you are troubled by anything in this book, the Samaritans
offer a free and supportive listening service. They can be
contacted by phone, letter, email or online chat.
Samaritans' website – https://www.samaritans.org
Freephone: 116 123
Welsh language free phone line: 0808 164 0123.

DEATH IS PART OF LIFE

Oral traditions from all over the world are full of stories giving shape to the very human wish to defy death – our own death and the deaths of others. The Western, British culture, in which we were both raised, is notoriously resistant to thinking about death, although evidence that we are mortal and our lifespan time-bound is all around us.

Oour tendency is to behave as though we will live forever. This is often part of the shock when someone close to us dies – at some level, we didn't really believe they would die, even if they were clearly very ill.

The story 'Death in a Nut' is, in many ways, our key text. A simple folk tale in the 'Jack stories' tradition, with a touch of humour as well as pathos, it carries at its heart a profound truth, that death and life are intertwined, and one could not exist without the other.

The story examines the denial or acceptance of death and their consequences. It carries to a logical conclusion the question 'What would happen if nothing died?' Jack learns that life extended beyond its purpose becomes unliveable and suffering inevitable.

The second story, 'An Unexpected Meeting', explores the same notion of 'the right time to die' from a different perspective. This is an Iraqi version of a common story motif, which again reminds us that death is invincible, and that there is no way to escape, trick or outrun it. There is a time and a season to all things, and death is an inevitable part of the circle of life.

1

DEATH IN A NUT

Imagine a cottage by the sea. Smoke curls from the chimney, chickens strut in the yard, fruit trees shade a pigsty.

That's Mary's home, where she lived with her son, Jack.

She had raised him from a baby on her own and, on the whole, she felt she had done a good job. He was even-tempered, kind to small children and animals, and useful for jobs that needed more than one pair of hands or required a bit of heavy lifting.

A cottage by the sea.

As Mary got older, she was more and more glad of his help. She was lucky with her health for a long time and neighbours complimented her on 'keeping so well', which she tried not to hear as a comment on her state of preservation, as though she were a pickle in a jar. But she knew, of course, that she was getting older, getting weaker. She tried to prepare Jack and get him thinking about what he would do when she was gone. But he always shied away from the subject. He just didn't want to think about it.

Which is why Jack had a shock the morning he came downstairs to find the fire out, the kettle cold, the chickens still cooped up. What was going on? Mary was always up before him. Then he heard her call from upstairs ...

He went back upstairs and put his head round her bedroom door. To his surprise, Mary was still in bed. She turned a pale face to him.

'Jack, love,' she said, 'I'm not too good today, not good at all. In fact, I think my time must have come. I've had a good life, and I'm not afraid to go ...'

Jack interrupted her. 'Mam, what are you talking about? Don't say such things! You've just got a bit of a cold, a touch of a virus. I'll get you a nice cup of tea and you'll soon be right as rain.'

'Well, Jack,' smiled Mary, 'I wouldn't say no to a cup of tea, but I do feel in my bones that Death will be calling for me today. And I do feel ready to go, though I'm sorry to be leaving you on your own ...'

'Mam, stop it now! Don't say such things. Don't even think them! Just lie there quietly and get better, and I'll make your tea.'

And Jack scarpered downstairs before he could hear any more. He did the jobs his mother usually did, and he did them reasonably well. He lit the fire, set the kettle, went out to see to the chickens and pig, and came back to the singing of the kettle.

He made the tea and took it upstairs. His mother's face looked grey and somehow transparent, and though he chattered away as though she would soon be fine, he felt a tightness round his heart that he had never known before.

Mary took his hands and made him meet her eyes. 'Jack,' she said, 'I've had a good life, and I'm not afraid to go. I know you'll be sad, but there's nothing wrong with a bit of grief, and in time you will be fine. Now it seems to me that Death will be coming for me sometime today, so if you'd rather not be here when he calls, why don't you go down to the beach for a while?'

Jack blustered and flustered for a bit, and even told his mother she was talking a load of rubbish, but eventually he agreed he would go and walk by the sea for a bit, though he insisted that by the time he came back she would be right as rain. He wouldn't say goodbye, though he did let his mother kiss him.

When he came back, he was looking rather pleased with himself. Mary was sitting at the breakfast table. She smiled at him, though her face still looked pinched.

'Are you feeling better, mam?' asked Jack, giving her a hug. She felt thin and fragile in his arms, but he shrugged off any doubts. He kissed her cheek. 'I said you would feel better after a bit of a rest, didn't I?'

'Well, yes, you did, Jack. I could have sworn that I was on my deathbed. But now ... well, I do feel a bit better. I got downstairs. Are you hungry?'

'Oh yes, mam. Are you?'

'Not really, Jack ...'

But Jack interrupted her.

'You need to build yourself up now, mam. I'll go out and get some eggs and scramble them for us.'

Jack went out and soon came back with a warm, brown egg in each hand. He carefully put one in a dish and tapped the other on the side of the pan. But it didn't crack. He tapped harder. Then harder. Nothing happened. He tried the second one. But he couldn't break that one either.

'This is very odd,' he said. 'I really fancied scrambled egg.'

'Well, never mind,' said Mary. 'There are some mushrooms and tomatoes in the larder. Would you like those on toast?'

So that's what he had.

But for the rest of the day, Mary kept contemplating those stubborn eggs; rolling them in her hands and surreptitiously dropping them on the floor when she thought Jack wasn't watching. She was wondering what was going on.

Because something definitely was going on.

This became clear the next day when Jack decided to go into the yard to kill their pig.

He was gone a long time. Mary looked up when Jack returned.

'I can't kill the pig,' he said in a bemused voice. 'The knife won't go in. It just bounces off.'

In the days that followed, strange stories began to circulate in the village.

Lowri Davies' pony broke its leg, and the vet simply couldn't put it down.

Little Jimmy Jones, fishing in the creek, got so upset by the way his trout flapped on the bank for half an hour that in the end, he threw it back.

Granfer Phillips, 92 and at death's door last week, seemed stuck on the threshold. He couldn't pass over, but he couldn't come back either.

No one, and nothing, could die. First it was a wonder. Then it was a mystery. But soon it became a crisis.

Stories began to circulate from the county abattoir: unkillable sheep, immortal swine, eternal cattle, coming in through one door and eventually being led out through another, alive and whole, when the place got too crowded to bring in more. Then news started coming from the area hospital: patients trapped in the grip of the most painful diseases; chronic infections going from bad to worse to unbearable; hopelessly premature babies clinging to life by the thinnest of threads that just wouldn't break.

Mary knew Jack so well that she could read him like a book. She became convinced, by his guilty shuffle whenever some new oddity was reported by the neighbours, by the way he wouldn't meet her eye when she tried to talk about her aches and pains, that there was a connection between her son and this strange new world in which nothing, and no one, could die.

She tried several times to broach the subject with him, but he always managed to find something urgent that needed doing, until one day she pinned him down.

Literally.

Mary got up early, groaning at the pains in her joints, and made two cups of tea. She took them into Jack's bedroom and sat down on the edge of his bed, deliberately trapping him under the tightly drawn covers. 'Jack,' she said, 'I've brought our tea up here this morning, so you and I can have a little talk.'

She looked at him meaningfully on the word 'talk', but he looked away, tugging at the counterpane, tight across his neck, and beginning to blether about thinking of going down to the beach to fish. But Mary was not to be deflected.

'Well, Jack, it's funny you should mention the beach, because I'd like to know a bit more about what happened on the beach, that day I woke up so poorly. What did you see, Jack? Or should I say, whom did you see?'

'No one, mam, no one. The beach was deserted – it was quite a grey day, if you remember. Like today, but I still think it's worth me seeing if I can catch something …'

'And if you do, Jack love, how will you kill it? Do you want to see the poor fish out of its element, struggling and suffocating, and no end to its suffering? Because that's what's happening, Jack, all around us. Not just to fish, but to all kind of things – every kind of thing. What happened on the beach that day, Jack? What did you do, to change the way things always were, the way they should always be?'

Jack squirmed and squiggled, but Mary's bottom was pulling the covers tight across his arms and legs, her eyes were boring into his. Even though he closed his eyes and turned his head, he knew she could see him – probably see his thoughts.

Jack cracked.

'His scythe and all.'

'O mam, I couldn't bear to think of losing you. I saw him coming, coming to get you, with his scythe and all, and ... and he thought he was so clever, but –' Here, Jack's voice grew more confident, and a gleam of triumph brightened his eyes. 'But I tricked him!'

And Jack told his mother how he had flattered Death into showing off.

'I tricked him! First, I asked if he could make himself big. He went really huge. He filled the sky! It was terrifying, to be honest, mam. But then I asked if he could go small as well. And he made himself tiny and helpless, so small he could fit into a nutshell. And I trapped him in it!'

'And what did you do with the nut, once you had trapped Death inside?' asked Mary, her voice gentle.

'I threw it into the sea, mam, so he couldn't take you, and then I came home, and you were alright!'

'But I'm not alright really, Jack, am I? I was weak and in pain that day, and if it was bad then, it's worse now. And there's no release for me, Jack, no peace. Don't you see, son, there is a time to live and a time to die, and if you push on past your time to go, then you suffer for it. I know you thought what you were doing was for the best, but it wasn't right, Jack. And now it isn't just me in trouble and pain, but every living thing whose time has come. It's true that Death sometimes comes before we are ready, and that is hard for everyone. But for those who are ready, it's much more terrible to be stuck in suffering and pain, when you could be free, believe me.'

Jack burst into sobs, and Mary gently reached out to him.

'Son, don't cry. I know you meant well, and I know you don't want me to go, but it *was* my time that day. And now it isn't just for you and me that the times are out of joint. You have to find a way to let Death back into the world. His work is as important as anyone's.'

She let him sit up then, and as they drank their tea, they talked heart to heart. And what they said is none of our business. But the upshot was an agreement that Jack would go back to the beach to look for Death and let him out.

So off he went.

Even as he reached the beach, Jack was thinking, 'This is ridiculous. This is impossible. It was a tiny hazel nut. I threw it into the sea. The great big sea ...'

He wandered hopelessly along the high tide line, kicking at lumps of seaweed. 'This is completely crazy,' he thought. 'I'll never find it.'

Then his belly tightened. 'But what if I don't? Everything that's going wrong: it's all my fault. All I cared about was myself, not what mam wanted.'

A sob rose in his throat, and he threw back his head to stare despairingly at the indifferent sky. Then he dropped his gaze once more to the infinite beach.

And he saw it. Balanced on the edge of a little dip in a grey stone: a hazel nut. But surely not *the* hazel nut? That would be too incredible, too unlikely.

Jack knelt down and looked at it closely. He saw a little hole where a creature had gone in to eat the meat and come out again. And he saw the splinter that he himself had pushed into that hole, to keep the other creature, the one he had tricked, inside.

Gingerly, he picked up the hazelnut and cradled it in his palm. Feeling rather foolish, he nonetheless addressed it earnestly: 'Is there anyone in there?'

A reply came, in a tinny little voice, 'Yes, of course, where else could I be? Jack, is that you? You tricked me into this. You are the only one who can let me out. Do it, Jack. Now, please.'

'But if I do, aren't you going to do something terrible to me, in revenge?' quavered Jack.

'Is there anyone in there?'

'Jack, I don't take revenge. I don't get emotional like humans. But I am getting tired of being cramped in here. And you know what a backlog of work I have got to deal with.'

'Yes, it's been really strange …'

Jack started to tell Death what the world had become without him.

But Death tutted impatiently. 'Jack, I don't need to hear your story. I just need to get on with things. Now stop chattering and do something useful, will you?'

Jack steeled himself, gripped the tip of the splinter and tugged it out of the hole. It was followed by a cloud of smoke, which quickly coalesced into a shadowless shadow on the sand.

Death harrumphed, shook out his robe, adjusted his cowl, inspected his scythe, got out his hourglass and tutted over it, then lifted his head and looked full into Jack's eyes. 'Jack,' he began, not unkindly. 'Do you understand things a bit more clearly now? Why life needs death and death needs life?'

'Yes,' muttered Jack, hanging his head. 'Yes, I do. I'm sorry for meddling in the natural order of things. Mam explained it to me. And I saw it with my own eyes, too. Sometimes Death is cruel, and sometimes kind. It isn't for me to interfere. But … but I do love my mam, and I don't know if I can manage without her.'

Jack broke into sobs at this point.

Death, who wasn't used to touching living flesh, patted him awkwardly on the shoulder. 'Jack, you'll be fine. Sad, but fine. And there's nothing wrong with being sad – or so they tell me. Feelings are a bit of a mystery to me. But I really must go now. I am miles behind. If it's alright with you, I'll start with your mam. She is a wise one, and ready to go. Why don't you stay on the beach for a while and watch the sunlight on the waves?'

'Yes, I will, and thank you, and I'm sorry,' mumbled Jack, looking out bleakly at the horizon.

'There's no need to apologise, only please, don't try it again. At first, I was grateful for the break, but doing nothing soon palled. And that nut was terribly cramped. But now I really must be off. Goodbye, Jack, until we meet again.'

Jack looked round in alarm at these words.

'No, don't worry,' said Death with a gravelly chuckle. 'Of course, eventually we will meet again, but not for a long, long time.'

'O, right. Goodbye then, Death,' said Jack. 'Until we meet again.'

And resolutely he fixed his eyes on the horizon, as Death set off towards his delayed appointment with Mary, who calmly welcomed him into the little cottage by the sea, with a last soft sigh.

2

AN UNEXPECTED MEETING

A rich merchant living in Baghdad sent his most trusted servant to the market to buy spices. As the man pushed through the crowds jostling around the colourful stalls, someone bumped into him. He turned to warn them to take care, only to find himself staring into the face of Death. Death looked straight into the horrified man's eyes, opened her mouth to speak and reached out her hand.

He did not stop to hear the words he dreaded. He turned and fled. When he got home he threw himself on his master's mercy. 'Lord, help me!' he begged. 'In the market place Death came for me. I saw that terrible face, close to mine. That bony hand reached out to clutch me … I am not ready to die! I beg you, lend me a horse so that I can outrun it!'

'When Death comes, it surely is our time, even though we may not think so,' said his master, who was a student of philosophy. 'But, since you are so afraid, I will do my best to help you. Take the fastest horse, with my blessing. Where will you go?'

'To Samara – thank you!' cried the servant, running from his master's presence straight to the stables.

A few moments later, the merchant heard the clatter of hooves over the cobbles. He sat and listened, until the sound grew fainter and faded away.

Four hours of fast riding.

'Hmm,' he said to himself, 'He has fled, and Samara is more than 130 kilometres away. But I ask myself whether anyone can escape Death when she truly comes for them. And now I must go to the market myself, if I am to have the spices I need.'

He rose with a sigh, and went down to the market, which was still in full swing. As he made his way towards the pungent stall where the finest spices were on display, the merchant saw that Death was still there in the marketplace. She passed unnoticed among the busy shoppers, but this merchant was a learned man, and he recognised her at once.

He was also a fearless man, for instead of imitating his servant and running away, he went straight up to Death and engaged her in conversation. 'Death,' he said, courteously but firmly, 'Only a short while ago, you gave my good servant a terrible fright. He told me that you reached for him, as though to speak.'

'Greetings, Lord,' replied Death politely. 'Indeed, no. The man mistook my intention. I had no time to explain before he fled, but I was not reaching for him. Rather, I was surprised to see him here in Baghdad. I have an appointment with him this evening in Samara, which is more than four hours of fast riding distant.'

'I see,' said the merchant. He paused, then spoke again.

'I think that, by the time you reach Samara, he will be there too. Truly, when the time comes, there really is no escaping you.' And he made a courteous bow to Death and left, contemplating, as he did so, the need to find a new servant.

CONNECTIONS BETWEEN THE DEAD AND THE LIVING

We asked fellow storytellers to recommend stories about death and dying to us. Our friend Tanya Batt in Aotearoa sent us the little story that begins this sequence. Tanya told us the story comes from Nigeria, from the tradition of the Nupe people. This theme, the choice between birth and death, is found in the stories of other cultures too: a stark reminder to humans that we can't have one without the other.

Paired with 'Why Stones Live Forever' is a story from the Islamic culture of Saudi Arabia. It also embodies the hard truth that death is inescapable, but in a very different mood and context. The pain of losing a child is given shape as the 'Pot of Sorrow'.

This story has great resonance for June. She writes:

When my brother died twenty-five years ago, I found solace in telling 'The Bedouin's Gazelle'. I felt my brother had been devoured by the ghoul Heroin. She was the monster who had eaten him. She had stolen him. The story gave a shape and a boundary to my grief. In telling the tale, I became both the Bedouin and his wife, tricking and comforting myself through the first shock and isolation of grief.

A key theme of the other two stories we have placed here is the enduring relationship between the living and the dead. 'The Companion' offers another powerful metaphor for the connections that we, the living, have with those who have died, foregrounding the debt that we owe them. In this story, that debt is reversed. Creating a written version of it for this collection has given us a chance to explore the complicated tropes of the story. It reflects a world where the use of violence to maintain power is seen as inevitable.

When telling such stories today, we have a choice:

We can reject the story as an aberration from a past time.

We can present the story as an artefact from a past time.

We can change what is unacceptable in the story and make it into a different story.

We can retell the story, incorporating an awareness of what is troubling in the story and offering the opportunity to explore it.

We've chosen the last course of action.

This story raises important questions in our world. Where there is still so much brutality – whose view is to be challenged? It's only the woman's view of the world that is questioned in this story. We're not called to question the lad's view. Why can't we see what she sees? Why can't he see what we see?

The lad is an innocent with a focussed desire. The companion has no sense of moral agency in carrying out the lad's wishes. He does not question the lad's goal. But we do.

The princess really doesn't seem very nice, but the idea that she can be thrashed into niceness isn't nice either. Who needs to be thrashed and shaken out of an old illusion into a new reality?

Surely both the lad and the princess do. We all do.

So, even with its cultural difficulties, this story is still worth contemplating. We hope you will agree.

This quartet of stories is completed by 'Grandfather's Flute', a story that June learned when storytelling in Mexico. It became part of the storytelling show, 'Sugar Skulls and Lovespoons', which she created to explore her relationship with departed family members. Its cheering resolution offers us hope, when plagued by regrets for words left unsaid and deeds undone, after death takes someone we care for. June finds a very personal resonance in the rituals of Dia de los Muertos, which are described in the story. She writes:

In October 2002 I spent a week telling stories to children in a school library in Guadalajara, Mexico. At the end of the week, the librarian invited me to her family celebration of Day of the Dead.

She and her family picked me up from my hotel on a bright Sunday morning. Our party included her husband, her mother and her little daughter, Angelita. We drove to the Guadalajara graveyard. The graveyard was full of activity, music and colour. There were huge cross-generational family groups as well as small groups like ours. A large crowd of young men and women were all sitting solemnly together, wearing expensive clothing and sunglasses, with a fantastic band playing. When I stared, my friend put her finger to her lips and shook her head. Members of a drugs cartel. Don't see them.

We were there to remember *Abuelo*. I had brought cake. I thought it was going to be a sort of picnic. My friend the librarian said, 'Thank you. Grandad loved cake.'

We walked through the trees and grave slabs, till we came to a small slab set flat in the grass. This was grandfather's stone. The family hung strings of paper flags in the branches of the trees all around. Beside *Abuelo*'s slab they set his photograph – a handsome, smiling old man. They set a mirror, marigolds, sweet plaited bread, my cake and a train whistle. My friend said, 'My dad worked for the railways all his life.'

We lit a candle. Grandmother, *Abuela*, watched and smiled. Then we all sat down quietly while my friend the librarian pulled out a flask. She unscrewed the top and I smelled coffee. She said, '*Abuelo* loved his morning coffee. Angelita used to take it to him, didn't you?'

Her little daughter nodded.

'He used to say, "I love my coffee, darling, and you always bring it. I'm really going to miss my coffee when I'm dead. You'll bring me my coffee, won't you, darling, when I'm dead?"

'And she does. She always does.'

My friend the librarian handed the flask to her little daughter, who took it and, walking around her grandfather's grave, carefully poured the coffee into the grass all around the edge.

As we walked back past other little slabs in the ground, I saw that on each there was a gift – a cigarette, a biscuit, a cup of Starbucks.

Since that time, on the Day of the Dead, I have made such altars for Robbie – a candle, a miniature of spirit, a coffee, a cigarette, his photograph.

3

WHY STONES LIVE FOREVER

At the very beginning of all times, there was no death. Everything lived forever. But alongside this, there was no birth either. How could there be? Things were in stasis: balanced, unchanging, unmoving, for a long, long time.

Things might still be like this today if it hadn't been for Turtle.

One day, Turtle said to her mate, 'Wouldn't it be nice to have some babies?'

'Babies? What do you mean?' asked Other Turtle.

'You know,' she said, 'Small turtles, young ones, that we could take care of. They would start off very small and sweet. And then they would grow.'

'Well, if you put it like that …' mused Other Turtle.

And before long, the two of them were looking up at Creator, who beamed down at them. Creator was very fond of all their creations and could well understand the appeal of bringing something new and innocent into the world.

Turtle said, 'Creator, we have come to ask you for babies.'

Creator replied, 'Well, you can have babies if you want them, but you must understand that, in order for something new to grow, something old must go. If you want to have babies in your lives, you will also have to have death. You will have to give up your immortality.'

The two turtles looked at each other, but it didn't take them long to see that they both felt the same.

'We would like the babies, please. We understand that means we can't live forever. We will have to make room for them.'

'Yes, that's just it,' said Creator, glad they understood. 'You'll have to make room.'

'O, no problem,' said the turtles together. 'Umm, where do we get them?

'What do you mean?' asked Creator, looking a bit puzzled.

'The babies,' they said. 'Where are they? Can we collect them today?'

Now Creator understood. A bit of explaining was needed.

'Well, the thing is,' said Creator, trying not feel embarrassed. 'You don't collect them. You make them.'

'Make them?' Now it was the turtles who looked a bit puzzled. 'How? Is there a kit?'

So Creator explained about sex.

And the turtles listened carefully. It was all a bit new. And in some ways surprising. But it sounded quite interesting. And they were a forward-thinking couple.

The Creator sketched out a few diagrams for them and explained that each of them would have a different role. 'But it's very much about working together,' said Creator. 'How do you feel about it all?'

The Turtles looked at each other again. They felt quite enthusiastic. They thanked Creator and said they felt pretty clear about what to do.

'And you won't forget, will you, about the bargain?' Creator reminded them. 'If you are going to bring babies into the world, you have to be prepared to die, in due course, to make room for them.'

'Yes, we understand,' said the turtles. 'Thank you very much. We can see that it makes sense.'

The bargain was agreed and the turtles went home. Pretty soon they had a clutch of eggs, and soon after that, a brood of cute little baby turtles.

When word got around, all the other animals were wild with curiosity to see the babies. And once they did see them, they were full of longing to have some of their own. Especially after the turtles mentioned how much they had enjoyed the sex part. In pairs, species by species, they went to Creator. In pairs they made the same bargain, trading Birth and Sex for Death.

Soon the world was full of the cheeping, squeaking, snoring, roaring, bleating, buzzing, snuffling and general cacophony made by new babies. And gradually death became part of the circle of life for all creatures: furred, finned, winged, shelled and naked.

They would start off very small.

Only the stones did not follow the trend. Even when Creator offered them children, the stones politely, but firmly, refused.

And this is why, of all things in creation, only stones are eternal and never-changing. Which is why the stones are the ones who hold and remember the stories of long ago. They do it for the rest of us, who don't have the long view.

4

The Bedouin's Gazelle

A Bedouin prepared to go hunting with his camel one morning. His wife bade him goodbye. 'Bring back a nice fat gazelle.'

As he rode out of the encampment, his young son ran after him, begging to be taken too. The Bedouin laughed. He was such a lovely child. The father hauled the youngster into the saddle in front of him and they rode to the wilderness together.

When he saw tracks on the earth, the Bedouin left his boy tending the camel. But as soon as he was gone, a huge ghoul crept from her cave in the rocks, stole up on the child and devoured him whole.

Returning and finding his son missing, the Bedouin followed the tracks on the earth to the cave where the ghoul was snoring. He killed the ghoul, slit open the belly and retrieved the body of his son. He wrapped the lad tenderly in the saddle blanket and returned home.

When his wife saw him, she cried out, 'What's that you've brought? I hope it's a fine fat gazelle.'

He saw her delight and could not find the words to tell her what she needed to know. Instead, he said, 'Yes. A young gazelle. But wife, this one is special. It can only be placed in a pot that has never been used to cook a meal of sorrow.'

'How strange. Well, our big pot is no good then,' said she. 'We used it last year for your father's funeral feast. Don't worry. I'll borrow one.' And off she went.

When she returned, she said, 'Husband, here is a problem. I could not find a single household with a pot that has never cooked a meal of sorrow. I have been listening to so many sad stories. Our poor neighbours! What are we to do about our gazelle?'

'Is it so?' said he. 'Yes. It seems all hearths have been visited by grief. Yes, wife. Yes, dearest. Now it is our turn to be visited by grief. Sweetheart, here is our little gazelle.'

'Here is our little gazelle.'

5

The Companion

There was once a young lad who had a dream. He dreamed of a lovely young woman, and in his dream, he lost his heart to her. When he woke the next morning, he remembered his dream vividly, and the lovely young woman even more vividly. Even though he had never met her, he was full of longing for her. That's what dreams can do …

Days passed, but he thought only of her. At last, he decided that there was nothing for it: either he must seek her out or he would surely pine away. He sold off everything he had and set out to wander the wide world in search of her.

Well, he walked a long and weary way, and as winter came on, he found himself in a strange, unfamiliar land, where the roads ran straight for mile upon mile. At last he came to a town. As he passed the church, he saw a great block of ice outside it. He saw, too, how everyone spat on it as they went by. His curiosity aroused, he took a closer look. Frozen inside the block of ice was a corpse!

Seeing the priest emerge from the church, he asked him, 'Father, what is that body doing there?'

'O, that is the corpse of a cheating rogue, who was executed some months ago, and the further punishment decreed for him was that he should never lie in consecrated land.'

'He must have committed a terrible crime, to receive such a harsh sentence,' said the lad.

'Indeed,' replied the priest. 'He had the wine shop here, and he used to water down the wine.'

Now, this did not seem like a hanging offence to the lad, so he ventured, 'But could he not now be laid in peace in a grave?'

The priest laughed. 'Who will break the corpse out of the ice?' he asked. 'And who will pay the grave digger to dig a grave and the sexton to toll the bell and the priest to take the service?'

'Well,' said the lad, 'I have some funds, and I will pay for all to be done as it should be done.'

'But what about the ale for the funeral wake?' asked the priest.

'Yes, I'll see to that too,' said the lad.

When this news went around the town, which it did fast enough, a couple of fellows came to chip off the ice, the undertaker fetched a coffin and laid the cold corpse in it, the grave digger dug the hole, the sexton tolled the bell and the priest spoke the words of the committal, while two muscle-bound men lowered the coffin into the ground. The funeral party at the graveside was small, only our lad and the priest, but the entire town turned out in force for free ale at the wake. By the time the lad had paid for all the drink, on top of the burial expenses, there was little enough in his pockets as he left the carousers behind him.

He took once more the long, straight road, and followed it away from that town, just as he had followed it there. When there was nothing as far as he could see but moors and mountains, he heard footsteps behind him. He turned to see another traveller making his way along the road, and soon the newcomer fell into step with him and they fell also, as travellers will, into polite conversation.

'I see we are headed in the same direction,' said the newcomer. 'Would you like a companion on your way, to shorten the road with agreeable talk?'

The lad declined politely, saying, 'I am happy enough in my own company, though thank you for the offer.'

'Then perhaps you need a servant to take care of your needs along the way?' persisted the stranger.

'Indeed, no,' laughed the lad. 'I am well used to taking care of myself, and in any case, I don't have money left to pay for such a luxury.'

'Listen,' said the stranger seriously, 'Take me as your companion. Believe me, you are going to need someone you can trust in life and death. And you can depend on me. I don't ask for any pay, and I will see to all my own expenses. Let me keep you company.'

The lad felt this was a genuine offer, and so he replied, 'Well, I don't know if it will be as perilous as you make out, but you seem an honest fellow. So, yes, on the basis you suggest, let us make an agreement to go on together.'

And so, they did.

They walked, side by side, on that long straight road, until they came to a mountain spur. Here, the companion stepped off the road and knocked on the side of the mountain. To the lad's surprise, a stone door creaked open, and there within the mountain stood an old woman, who beckoned them in and pointed towards a chair.

'Come in and sit down, my boys,' she said. 'You must be weary from your travels.'

The lad stepped forward gratefully, but his companion stopped him with a warning look and a slight shake of the head. He spoke harshly to the old woman, 'You intended to trap us, but instead, you shall sit there as long as I wish it.'

And with that, he stepped forward and pushed the old woman down onto the chair. She swore and spat but couldn't get up. She was trapped, just as they would have been.

Now the companion began to look around the house. The lad stood in confusion, but the companion's search seemed purposeful, and he made a satisfied little noise as he caught sight of a sword that was hanging over the door.

'We'll have that,' he said to the old woman, indicating the sword. 'And after it's in my hand you shall go free from that chair.'

'No, no, not that!' screeched the old woman in alarm. 'You can have whatever you ask for, if you will set me free, but not that. That is my Three Sister Sword, and I cannot give it away!'

'Whether it is your Three Sister Sword or your Ten Sister Sword makes no difference to me. Either we shall have it, or you will sit there until the mountain crumbles around you.'

The old woman ranted and raved, and then begged and pleaded that he choose something else, anything else – but the companion was implacable, and stoutly refused each more generous offer that she made.

Still the lad watched, all in confusion, until at last, the old woman relented and agreed they should have the sword.

With her reluctant permission, the companion took down the sword, opened the door to the outside world and beckoned the lad to go in front of him. Turning back as he stepped over the threshold, he called to the woman, 'In a little while the chair will set you free, but we will be gone and you are not to follow.'

And with that, he slammed the door and they went on their way.

As they walked, the companion wedged the Three Sister Sword into his belt. But he explained nothing of what had happened or why, leaving the lad to carry his confusion with him.

And so, they went on, until the companion stopped at a sheer rock face that, to the lad, looked no different from any other bit of geology they had passed, and once again he rapped on the rock. And a door opened. There stood an old woman, very similar to the first old woman, though, if possible, even older, and she too welcomed them inside and indicated that they should take a seat. 'For you must be weary of walking,' she said.

Well, he was weary, but, remembering what had gone before, the lad hesitated, and while he stood there dithering, the companion pushed the old woman onto the chair, declaring, 'No, you shall sit there, not him or me, and you shall sit till the end of time, unless I say otherwise.'

And as the woman writhed and swore, he began to search the place, with the air of one who knows what he is looking for. He opened and looked through every drawer in the place – and there were many – until he caught sight of a flash of gold, and triumphantly pulled a ball of golden yarn from the back of a cupboard.

'We will have this, and you shall go free,' he said.

'No, not that, you cannot have that,' wailed the woman. 'That is my Three Sister Ball and I cannot be without it.'

'Then you shall stay stuck in that seat till the skies fall down,' said the companion pitilessly, 'For this is what we want and this is what we will have.'

So she had to let him have his way.

Reassuring her that, when they were far enough away, the chair would release her, the companion tucked the Three Sister Ball into his pocket and ushered the bemused lad back out onto the path. He strode jauntily away and the lad followed after, feeling sure that his companion had a plan, but with no idea what it might be.

When they had penetrated even further into the mountains the companion stopped for a third time. This time, the lad was not surprised by what happened next, and sure enough, he was soon following his companion into a third, really old woman's rock-bound den.

Here, yet again, there was a malevolent invitation to sit upon an apparently harmless chair, and here again the companion made sure it was the old woman who was soon stuck there. Once she was trapped, he started to search the place, while the lad wondered idly what object he wanted this time. When the companion took down a battered old hat from a hook on the door, the lad felt quite disappointed. It wasn't a weapon. It wasn't made of gleaming gold. What was so special about the hat?

But this old woman too bewailed the choice. 'That is my Three Sister Hat and I cannot let it go.'

Whether she would, or whether she would not, in the end she had to agree that the companion could take it, for otherwise he threatened to leave her on the chair till the crack of doom.

Soon enough they were on their way again, leaving the old woman with the promise that, once they were safely away, she would be able to leave the chair. The companion folded the Three Sister Hat into his pouch and strode along, the lad following behind, wondering what on earth would happen next.

After a long, long way of walking, they reached a ravine, with a fast-flowing stream rushing through it far below, between sheer sides. There was no way to get across. The companion took the golden ball out of his pocket and said to the lad, 'Now you will see the value of the Three Sister Ball.'

With that, he threw the ball across the ravine so hard that it struck the other side and bounced right back to his hand, leaving a trail of thread across the gulf and back again. He threw it again and again, and each time a trail of thread was added, until the ball was all used up and a rope bridge, narrow and swaying, stretched across the ravine from one side to the other. On that precarious bridge, they crossed safely to the other side, but as the lad sank down in relief on solid ground once more, the companion turned to him with urgency in his face. 'Be quick now and wind the yarn back up, for those three sisters are not far behind us, and if they once cross over, there will be no escape from their vengeance.'

The lad jumped to his feet and stared back over the ravine. Sure enough, he could see a cloud of dust in the distance, as though something or someone was heading towards them at speed. He felt a shiver of fear, grabbed the end of the yarn and began to wind it up as fast as he could. He wound and he wound, and all the while their pursuers got nearer and nearer, until, while the last thread was still trailing across the gulf, they reached the far side.

They leapt as one out into the void, reaching to grab hold of the trailing yarn. The lad wound faster than he ever thought he could, and the end of the thread flicked tantalisingly out of the grasp of the first of the three women. She stretched out for it, screaming curses, but the lad, with every ounce of strength that he had, twirled and spun the ball in his hands and the loose end was drawn up and in.

The three women, having nothing to catch hold of, fell down, down, down into the fierce-flowing water of the torrent below and were swept away, faster than thought.

The lad gaped into the abyss. His companion took the untidy bundle of yarn from him, neatened it up, put it in his pocket and started to walk. Still shivering with shock after such a narrow escape, the lad followed.

A few days of eventless walking after that, the companion broke the silence and said, 'Soon we will reach the castle where she lives: the princess you dreamed of. When we get there, you must go in and tell the king what you dreamed and what you want.'

The lad nodded, suddenly dry-mouthed. Sure enough, the next day found them walking up a long avenue that led to a castle set among rocks and crags.

The lad did and said as his companion had instructed him and they were both warmly received. At dinner time, the lad approached the high table and saw, seated beside her father the king, the young woman of his dreams. He was overcome with love, though it is hard to say what was in the princess's heart just then.

Notwithstanding, she greeted him warmly, bade him sit beside her, and smilingly engaged him in conversation. He told her why he was there and she stared boldly at him, declaring that she liked him well enough.

'However,' she said, 'We have the custom here that every suitor for my hand – and there have been many –' she added, her eyes modestly downcast, '… every suitor must undertake three trials to determine whether he is worthy.'

The lad braced himself and declared that he was ready to attempt the most difficult or dangerous tasks in the world to prove the depth of his devotion.

'Ah,' laughed the princess, 'It is not so hard, though perhaps hard enough. All I ask is that you take care of these for me and return them safe to my hand tomorrow at midday.' And she took from her pocket a little pair of gilded scissors and gave them to him.

'But,' she continued, still with the same happy smile, 'If you fail, the penalty is to be drawn and quartered – that is the law – and your body and head will be set on separate stakes around the entrance to the castle, like the old bones you saw as you arrived.'

To be honest, the lad had seen no such thing, and if he had, perhaps this story would have been much shorter; but, being now committed, he took the shining scissors and put them in his pocket, thinking all the while, 'Well, the penalty is truly harsh, but the test does not seem so hard. Perhaps she really likes me and wants me to succeed …'

So caught up was he in his fantasy and the charm of her gaze and the flattery of her attention that he never noticed when she skilfully picked his pocket and took back the

scissors, before ever he left the table. It was only when he
and the companion were alone in their rooms that evening
that he realised that his pockets were empty. After frantically turning them out over and over again, he sank down
in despair.

But his companion patted him on the shoulder and said
only, 'Well, well, let's see if I cannot get them for you again.'

With the Three Sister Sword in his belt and the Three
Sister Hat in his pocket, the companion went down to the
stable. There was tethered the princess's billy goat, and this
was one of those breeds – you know the sort – that can fly
through the air faster than they can travel by land.

Oh, and they can talk, if forced.

Well, the companion slapped the goat between its horns
with the flat of the Three Sister Sword, and asked, 'When
does the princess ride out to see her lover?'

The billy goat rose into the air.

The billy goat at first refused to tell, but another blow from the Three Sister Sword encouraged it to change its mind, so that it bleatingly admitted that the princess would come at eleven o'clock. The companion left it in peace after that, but he didn't leave the stable. Instead, he put on the Three Sister Hat, which at once made him invisible, and he waited quietly in a corner till the princess came in, on the stroke of eleven.

She rubbed the billy goat with ointment from a great hollow horn and said, 'Away, away, over moor, over mountain, to my true love in the cavern who waits for me tonight.'

Immediately, the billy goat rose into the air, the princess leaping astride its back. The invisible companion threw himself on behind the princess and away they flew through the night air.

It was not long before they came to a cross-mountain. The princess knocked on the face of the rock and they all passed through a stone door into the heart of the mountain, where the princess's lover, a troll, squatted in wait for her.

'What news?' he asked, when they had finished their slobbery and quite revolting kiss of greeting.

'Well, my dear,' she laughed, 'Another suitor is come, and I have set him a task, as you taught me.'

'And what task did you set?'

'To keep and care for these scissors, which I took from him so easily he never noticed they were gone,' she laughed, holding up the scissors and kissing the troll again. 'You shall keep them, not he!'

The troll and the princess laughed at the thought of the fate of the lad, and the troll smirked, 'Oh, I'll keep them safe enough.'

With that, he opened an iron chest with three locks. But as he placed the scissors inside, and before he could lock the triple locks, the companion reached out his invisible hand

and took the scissors. And neither of them saw him, because of the magic of the Three Sister Hat.

So the troll locked the chest and hid the key for nothing.

Once midnight had struck, the princess bade goodbye to her lover and set off home again. The companion rode behind her on the goat, and neither girl nor goat was any the wiser.

Next day, about midday, the lad was summoned to lunch in the great hall. The princess and her father were waiting, but this time there were no friendly smiles, no flirting. The princess hardly looked at him. But when the meal was over, she put on a smile and said, 'Now, do you have those scissors I asked you to keep so carefully yesterday?'

'Indeed, I do,' replied the lad. 'And here they are!'

He slammed the scissors down onto the table so hard that they drove into the wood. The princess was as vexed as could be, but she made herself soft and gentle, and mildly said, 'Since you have kept my scissors so well, I am sure the second task will be no trouble to you at all. Take my golden ball of yarn and keep it safe for me until I ask for it, tomorrow at noon. But if you lose it, your life will soon follow. That is our law.'

She gave him a familiar-looking golden ball. Once again, he put her gift into his pocket, and once again, she began to charm and flirt with him, so that he forgot all about it. Then it was easy for her to pick his pocket and relieve him of the prize. Soon after that, with many sweet words, she sent him off.

In their chamber, he told the companion all that had taken place, and his friend asked, 'And do you have the golden ball she gave you?'

He felt in his jacket pocket, then in the other pocket, then through all his pockets in turn, over and over, until at last, he was forced to admit that, no, he did not have the golden ball and he couldn't think how he had lost it, and now his life would be forfeit.

He looked ready to weep, but the companion urged him, 'Bear up, my friend. I'll see if I can find it for you.'

Off he went, down to the stable, with the Three Sister Sword and the Three Sister Hat. He used the first to whack the billy goat so hard that it turned head over heels, and the second to make himself invisible once the goat had told him to expect the princess at midnight.

At the first stroke of twelve, in she came, and quickly greased the billy goat from the horn of ointment, saying, 'Away, away, over hill, over hollow, to my true love in the cavern, who waits for me tonight.'

Kissing and cuddling in a quite revolting way.

Up went the billy goat with the princess on its back, and on jumped the companion in his Three Sister Hat, and neither princess nor goat noticed that anything was amiss.

Soon, the princess and her troll lover were kissing and cuddling in a quite revolting way, and not long after that, she was gleefully telling the troll how she had once again taken from the lad the object which he had sworn to keep till the morning. 'But I don't understand how he got the scissors back,' she said, thoughtfully. 'And they *were* my scissors, there's no doubt of that. You must find somewhere much safer to keep this ball of yarn, my darling. We can't risk him succeeding a second time.'

'I know just the thing,' said the troll smugly. 'We'll destroy it.' He took the ball of yarn from her hand and threw it in a long arc towards the fire blazing in the centre of the cavern.

But just as the ball began to fall into the flames, the invisible companion reached out his invisible hand and caught it, sliding it into his invisible pocket so quickly that it disappeared from view, just as if it had fallen into the fire.

The princess caressed the troll and murmured how much she admired his ingenuity, as well as his many other excellent qualities, while the troll preened and lapped up the praise. The companion, meanwhile, sighed and fidgeted invisibly in the corner, until at last, he could hitch a ride home on the billy goat's back.

When the goat was in its stable and the princess was in her bed, the companion crept into the lad's room and quietly put the ball of yarn beside him on the pillow.

At midday, the lad presented himself in the great hall of the castle. When the princess charmingly asked for her golden ball of yarn, he was gratified to see the astonished look on her face as he handed her the golden ball. 'So,' she said, slowly, 'You have done well. There is just one task left for you. Are you ready to try it?'

The lad, delighted at being over halfway to his goal, nodded enthusiastically.

'All I ask is this, and if you are successful, we shall be married: tomorrow at midday, bring me the thing I am thinking of now!' And she screwed up her brow and gazed into mid-air, to demonstrate that she was indeed thinking of something at that very moment.

The lad stumbled from the table and staggered upstairs, to bemoan his fate to his sympathetic companion. 'Now I am lost, for how on earth could I ever guess what she was thinking of at that moment? O, cruel fate …'

'Well,' said the companion soothingly, 'Perhaps there is another way. Leave this one to me, too.'

Though the lad felt as though the hours crept past, at last he was in bed and somewhat surprisingly, given the circumstances, he soon fell asleep.

Then the companion went down to the stable, where he whacked the billy goat with the sword, until it told him that the princess would ride out at one in the morning.

Sure enough, on the dot, she came into the stable carrying the horn of grease. After liberally smearing the goat, she declaimed, 'Away, away, over bog, over briar, to my true love in the cavern, who waits for me tonight.'

Away they flew, with their invisible passenger. But this time, the companion did not content himself with sitting quietly. Instead, he buffeted both goat and princess with the flat of the Three Sister Sword, until they cried out – or bleated – in pain, and the princess was convinced that the wind must be full of flying debris, which had injured her. Indeed, she complained bitterly to her lover, showing him the beginnings of some impressive bruising.

'And what's more,' she moaned, 'This suitor somehow managed to bring me the ball of yarn. How could that be? I saw you throw it into the fire.'

'I was thinking of your own dear head!'

Both were nonplussed – though, in truth, it doesn't take a lot to nonplus a troll. But then the princess cheered up. 'Still,' she said, 'I have set him a task that truly will be impossible this time: I told him he must bring me the thing I was thinking of at that moment – and I was thinking of your own dear head!'

They both burst out laughing, and the princess embraced the troll's ugly head lovingly, while in the corner the invisible companion smiled grimly and hefted his Three Sister Sword. The ill-matched pair carried on cackling and canoodling till it was nearly dawn, and the princess then began to make ready to leave.

'But I am afraid to go alone,' she confessed. 'The journey here was so brutal tonight. You must come with me as far as the castle door, to make sure I am safe.'

Well, the troll agreed to do that, so they both went down to the stable, where the troll brought out his own billy goat and his own horn of grease. They mounted their two flying goats and the companion jumped up behind the troll, in order to bash and batter him all the way home.

This rough treatment by an unseen cause convinced the troll that the princess did indeed need protecting, and he went with her right to the door of the castle stable, where she kissed him tenderly, waved goodbye and led her goat into its stall. As soon as she was out of sight, the companion drew out the Three Sister Sword, whacked off the troll's head in one clean sweep, kicked the body down the slope and set the goat loose on the hillside. Then he ran up to the lad's room, woke the lad, and threw down the troll's head, saying, 'This is what she was thinking of.'

The lad stared in horror at the grisly trophy, but he did not doubt his companion's word. And indeed, when he placed it carefully on the table in front of the princess, though she went pale and swayed as though she would faint, she could not, in all honesty, deny that this was indeed what she had been thinking of. She agreed in a quiet voice that the tasks had been completed and that their marriage would be arranged forthwith.

It was a strange ceremony, for the bride was as cold and pale as stone, though the groom trembled with joy. When the feast was eaten, and it was time for the bride and groom to retire to bed, the companion took the new husband aside. 'My friend, whatever you do, you must not lie down with the princess before you have undone the enchantment that the troll placed upon her long ago. If you do not, she will kill you and tear you to pieces.'

The groom's enthusiasm for his wedding night waned enormously in that moment.

'Is there anything I can do?' he whispered tremulously.

'This is what you must do,' said the companion, and proceeded to give him strict, and very complicated, instructions.

The companion told him how to strip off the troll skin that her lover had cast over the princess. 'Only when her true self is revealed will the spell which made her deadly, be overturned. You must beat her with birch twigs to flay the troll skin. Then you must dunk her in a tub of whey and scrub her till the troll skin is all rubbed away. Then you must wash her in a tub of buttermilk, to be sure that all traces of troll are gone. Only after all this can you bathe her in a tub of new milk. Then she will at last be returned to her true self and her own will.'

The lad promised to do everything his friend had told him, and immediately ordered some rather unusual accoutrements for the bridal chamber.

At last, he and his new bride were all alone in their room, but by the time she came to bed in her new negligee, he was pretending to be asleep. The princess poked his shoulder with her finger. He did not stir. She tickled his nose and cheeks, but he did not move. She tugged at his hair, but he did not budge.

Satisfied that he was fast asleep, she slid out a butcher's knife from under her negligee and, taking hold of his hair to pull back his head, prepared to slit his throat. But he jumped up, grabbed her wrist and forced the knife from her hand.

Then he set about the tasks the companion had described.

Let us draw a veil over the flogging and the scrubbing, which all seem distastefully violent to me, though clearly indispensable to the plot. Suffice it to say that, by the morning, the princess's skin was pink and shiny from all the exfoliation she had undergone, and her mind was clear and free of the last traces of the troll's evil power. She gazed at the lad as if for the first time, and lost her heart to him then, just as he had lost his to her in his dream, so long ago.

Soon after that, the lad and the princess set out for his home. The companion went with them, of course, and he brought for them the gold and treasure that the troll had hoarded, strapped to the backs of the flying billy goats, now earthbound by the weight of the treasure.

And all seemed to be coming to a happy ending, for the lad and the princess were truly in love. But when they were at last in sight of home, the companion bade farewell to his friend, and the lad's face fell. 'But I thought we would stay together,' he stammered.

'No, I must go now.'

'At least come as far as the house, to drink the homecoming ale with us,' begged the lad.

'No, I cannot, I am sorry.'

'But you must let me reward you, for all you have done for me,' he pleaded.

The companion refused to take anything, but the lad implored and insisted, until at last they agreed that, though the companion would take nothing now, he would return in five years, when the lad would divide everything he possessed equally between them.

And then he turned and strode away.

The lad missed his friend, but being a newly married, and newly wealthy, man soon took his mind off this loss. He focussed instead on all he had gained. The princess and he were happy together, and when a little boy was born to them, their joy felt complete.

As the five years were coming to an end, the lad began to look with anticipation for his companion, and he set to, dividing the wealth into two equal portions. 'One for him and one for us,' he told the princess, and she agreed that the companion indeed deserved an equal share in their good fortune.

When the companion did arrive, looking no different from when they had parted so long before, they greeted him warmly and lovingly. He returned their affection. The lad led him into the great store room of their fine home. Two heaps of treasure were piled up there.

'My friend,' said the lad, 'I have divided everything, and this is your share.'

'An equal share in all you have?' asked the companion.

'Indeed,' replied his friend.

'But I think there is something else. Have you and your wife not had a child since I left? Would it not be fair to share the child equally between us?' And he held out the Three Sister Sword.

The lad's face went pale, but he did not hesitate. He owed more than he could ever repay to this man.

He grasped the hilt of the Three Sister Sword and called his son to him. Trustingly, the child trotted to his father, who raised the sword above his head, tears coursing down his face. The princess stared aghast, and then stepped forward and cried out, 'Take him! Take the boy!'

The companion looked from one to the other and shook his head. 'Keep everything you were prepared to give away, especially the joy of your little son,' he said gently. 'I do not need a thing, for I am a soaring spirit now, thanks to you.

'I was the cheating shop owner in the block of ice outside the church door, and I became your companion and helped you, because you gave all you had, to free me from the ice and give me a decent burial.

'And so, I was allowed to be with you, to help you all I could, in order to atone for my sins. And I have been granted permission to come back to see you just once more, to tell you the secret of who I really am. You have shown me that our friendship was true, and that you are prepared to do anything for my sake, as I have been for yours. But now I am going to my rest, and you will never see me more. Thank you for your friendship.'

'And thank you for yours,' cried the lad, in a voice choked with emotion.

As he watched, his companion walked away, vanishing into thin air.

6

GRANDFATHER'S FLUTE

There was once an *abuelo*, a grandfather, who lived with his granddaughter at the edge of the village beside the desert. He was a farmer. His great love was music. He played a bone flute.

It wasn't an easy thing for a working man to bring up a little baby girl, but he did it. Each morning he would make his coffee, then he would wash and dress and feed his darling. He'd bundle her up, tie her onto his back and carry her to his field. There, he'd lay her in the shade of the tree, and she would kick and coo and listen to the sound of his spade in the soil.

When she was old enough, she'd help him to water and weed. Each evening he'd cook, and he'd tell her stories. She would fall asleep to the sound of his flute. He always played the flute. She wouldn't sleep unless he played the flute.

Then he'd light his pipe and watch over her as she slept.

So, the girl grew in the steady cycles of the years – earth, corn, stories, tobacco and the music of the flute. She grew and blossomed. The grandfather diminished and weakened.

Now it was grandfather who wakened to the smell of coffee. The girl would bring him the coffee. She helped him wash and dress. He watched her work in the field.

But when night came, it was as it had always been. When grandfather had eaten, he played the flute and she would fall asleep to the sound of his music.

One night the grandfather died.

Good neighbours gathered round the granddaughter.

Together, they helped her to prepare the necessary ceremony – the washing and cooking, the cleaning. But it was
her duty, and her duty alone, to prepare the little package
of possessions that her grandfather would need to take with
him on his journey to the otherworld, to the land of the
dead, which lies beyond the Green Gates of Dawn.

Carefully, she gathered the things that were necessary
to his being: his coffee cup and his flute. She placed them
on brightly coloured woven fabric. She packed his pipe
with his tobacco, lit it and blew a breath of sacred smoke
over the objects. Then she emptied the pipe and placed it
among his possessions on the fabric and folded them into
a travelling bundle for her grandfather to carry with him
to the otherworld. She tied them tight with twine. Then
she joined the villagers as they carried her grandfather in
procession to the desert.

There, among the agave, the yucca and the prickly pear,
they laid him down. She placed the bundle of his possessions on his heart. The elder threw back his head and called
into the darkening sky. Everyone looked upwards and, high
above, they all saw a dot circling in the blue of space and
spiralling downward. They knew this was Zapilota, Little
Vulture, answering the call of the elder, coming for *Abuelo*.
All was as it should be.

Little Vulture would carry grandfather up to the Green
Gates of Dawn, where Wiracucha, Big Vulture, would throw
open the gates and welcome him in.

They said their goodbyes, lit their torches and turned
for home.

Here it was on the table.

Her friends and neighbours accompanied her to her hut, but as they entered, she saw, to her horror, that there on the table was her grandfather's beloved flute. She was sure she had packed it into the otherworld bundle. Yet, here it was on the table.

Her friends tried to calm her. 'It's an understandable mistake. You were upset. Your *abuelo* will forgive you. Your *abuelo* is resourceful. He has already forgiven you. He will make a new flute. Someone will lend him a flute. Be at peace.'

But she could not be at peace. '*Abuelo* played his flute every day. How will my grandfather be at peace when he cannot play his flute? How can I ever be at peace knowing my grandfather cannot play his flute? How can I be at peace when my grandfather is not at peace?'

She seized the flute and stumbled back along the desert road by moonlight, to the place where he had been laid. But she was too late. There was no trace of her grandfather. Zapilota had already carried *Abuelo* away. There was nothing there but moonlight and the sound of the night crickets and the breeze in the brush.

Then she threw back her head and she uttered the cry she'd heard the elder give – one long, summoning cry into the sky.

Far above, she saw a dark circling dot in the moonlight, descending, spiralling, hovering. It was Zapilota. Little Vulture had come at the call of the dead.

He landed clumsily on a cactus, eyed her, and said, 'I come for the dead.'

She bowed her head. 'You come.'

'You don't look dead.'

'Well, no. I'm not dead.' she said. 'But even so, I ask you to take me. I must travel through the Green Gates of Dawn and go to the land of the dead.'

Zapilota said, 'It can't be done if you're not dead.'

She said, 'But I must go to the land of the dead to give my grandfather his flute.' And she showed him her grandfather's flute.

Zapilota was very interested by the sight of the flute. His whole attitude changed. He said, 'Ah! The flute! I love the music of the flute! If only I could sing that song. I would do anything to play the music of the flute.'

Now, the truth was that the girl had never played her grandfather's flute. But she said, 'I could teach you, and if I do, will you take me to the Green Gates of Dawn?'

'If you teach me, I will.'

He carried her through the upper regions of the sky to the Green Gates of Dawn. There stood Big Vulture.

'Are you dead?' asked Big Vulture.

'If you teach me, I will.'

Little Vulture answered for her, 'Well, no, she's not. But living, as she is, she has offered us a gift. She will teach us the music of the flute to gain entry.' He nodded at the girl, and she showed Big Vulture the grandfather's flute.

Big Vulture changed his attitude. He said, 'Ah! The flute! I love the music of the flute. Yes! If you can play this flute and teach us, then, living as you are, you may come and go as you wish. Now play. Play!'

The girl thought, 'I have never played my grandfather's flute, but since the day that I first saw light, I have heard the music of my grandfather's flute. I know all his tunes. His music is in my heart. Surely, as I am my grandfather's granddaughter, I can play his music.'

Gently, she placed her lips on the flute and blew her heart's breath into it.

Sad to say, it takes more than a good ear and a good heart to make a musician. It takes practice. She couldn't play.

There was a breathy whistle and a hoot and a squeak from the flute and then terrible wordless anger from both vultures, Big and Little. Big Vulture slammed shut the Green Gates of Dawn and the girl was trapped inside. The life she was to have lived was outside. It was lost to her.

She turned from the gates and began to wander through the otherworld.

For a long time, she wandered alone in the diffuse blue light of the otherworld. But, at last, she found her grandfather, sitting beneath a tree. He recognised her at once and she him and they were delighted to be reunited.

Then he said, 'Oh darling granddaughter! Is it so soon? Have you died so soon?'

'Well, *Abuelo*, no.' She told him the whole story and then she gave him his flute.

He said, 'Dear child, thank you for this gift, but the sacrifice is too great. You have a long life ahead of you and I shall see that you will live it.' Then he breathed a long note into his flute and the sweet sound of it filled the otherworld. On the instant, they were surrounded by all the musicians of the otherworld. Together, they played a great music.

The sounds of the grandfather's band could not be silenced. The music penetrated through the cracks and hinges and joints and gaps of the Gates of Dawn and travelled to the world beyond. The sounds reached each human ear and when each ear heard, each heart opened and each mind remembered.

Each one reached out for a sweet, a marigold, a memento. Each one lit a candle for the remembered loved one and went to the graveyard to sit and honour. Great crowds gathered, and as they did, in the otherworld, the strength of all those memories pressed open the Great Green Gates of Dawn.

The power of remembrance pushed open the gates of the otherworld. All those souls within became birds, and the spirit birds flew through the Green Gates of Dawn to return to their descendants.

The girl saw that her grandfather, too, had become a bird, as had all the musicians of the otherworld – rising up and singing. And she was flying with them, carried on her grandfather's broad back, just as she had been as a child. And all the music was playing, and all the spirits were singing their songs wholeheartedly.

But all those spirits would have been lost in the great, wide wilderness of space and time if it had not been for the bright points of light and the murmur of voices in the distance far below. The descendants were lighting candles and singing songs and telling stories. They were telling 'Cavaleros' – the funny little stories of the lives of their ancestors. They were singing the songs that commemorated their ancestors. They were laughing and they were crying over the stories of the past lives of their loved ones. And the spirits saw the light and heard the laughter.

The spirit birds followed the light and sound, and so did the grandfather. They perched in the trees and on the stones around the candles and the stories and the gifts and the food. The girl alighted from her grandfather's back. They shared sweet bread. They sang a song or two together.

Before morning, she bade him goodbye. He and his fellow spirits flew back up through the Green Gates of Dawn to the otherworld.

Since then, on every Dia de los Muertos, the people have lit candles and offered little gifts – a delicious cake, a special photograph, the scent of coffee, a favourite tune, a funny little story – all to call the loved ones home.

DEFYING DEATH

Here are two stories from very different times and cultures, both exploring the possibility of defying death. The first story describes the powerful urge to bring back one who is lost. The second tells of the determination to challenge and conquer death.

'To the Mountains …' is the Siberian story of a sister grieving for her dead brother. She draws on her grief – and the help of her wonderful horse – to find the strength to search for him and bring him back from the dead. June writes:

Many years ago, I found this story in a book on the shelves of a little annexe of the British Library. I photocopied the story but did not take note of the book's title or author. I did not realise at the time how significant the story would become to me.

It is significant to me for several reasons.

It shaped my development as a storyteller. I began working on it long before my brother died. That phase of the work was to do with craft. I had to shape and structure something that was manageable for the listeners and for me as the teller. Then I realised it wasn't working and had to decide whether there was something worth pursuing. Finally, I had to raise the stamina to start all over again, to go right back to the beginning to reshape and restructure.

After my brother's death, the story took on a talismanic significance. I was telling it for him. The story did not represent our relationship, yet it provided the opportunity for a sort of displaced meditation on our relationship, which still existed beyond death. The ability to return again and again to the story arose out of that energy and relationship, so that I was able to work for a prolonged period, adding such elements as the two embedded fables of 'Thirteen Parts of Wisdom' and 'Truth in the Mountain Cave', which are imported from elsewhere. At last, it felt finished.

Fiona writes:

'Inanna's Descent to the Underworld', the story we have paired here with 'To the Mountains ...', is a very early story, among the oldest known tales in the world. It comes from Ancient Sumer, one of the world's first developed civilisations and the culture that has the best claim to have invented writing. At some time between 3000–5000 BCE, this story, almost certainly originally an oral tale, was preserved, by being written down. The script invented then is known as cuneiform, and it was pressed with a pointed tool into wet clay tablets, which were then sun baked to harden them. So, a Sumerian library, such as the Library of King Ashurbanipal, the great doors of which can be seen in London's British Museum, contained, not books or rolls of papyrus or vellum, but clay tablets, each about the size of a scribe's palm, made from the abundant mud of two great rivers. These rivers, the Tigris and the Euphrates, gave the

name Mesopotamia, 'between the rivers', to the land that
is now called Iraq.

I have been learning about the culture of Ancient
Sumer for more than thirty years. Unlike June, who
worked on the first tale in this pairing before finding
its deeper significance to her own life experience, I discovered 'The Descent of Inanna' through the acute grief
I experienced at my mother's death, as explained in the
introduction to this collection.

My mother and I were involved in a road traffic
accident, which proved fatal to her, while I escaped with
barely a scratch. A particularly troubling aspect of my
bereavement was the need to come to terms with my
responsibility, as the driver of the car, for her death. I felt
cut off from, and dead to, the comfort of others, especially
because of my feelings of guilt and remorse. I was in sore
need of a way to live with a great loss in my life. Finding a
truly ancient text that described so accurately my feeling
of isolation gave me a sense of kinship to Inanna, even
though our stories are separated by hundreds of miles and
thousands of years. The version that I developed, though
very personal, is redolent of the insights of Alida Gersie
and the poetry of Diane Wolkstein.

Surely, one of the most valuable aspects of traditional
tales is this: that they embody universal human truths that
transcend time and cultures and remind us that we are not
alone, that others have suffered as we suffer now, and that
they have come through to the other side. When Inanna
returns from the Underworld, although there is, as always,
a price to be paid, she is able to take up the threads of her
life: they were not severed, merely tangled for a while. And
this, too, was my experience at last, though it took me
rather longer than the three days and nights of the myth.

1

To the Mountains for a Brother, Through the Furnace for a Lover

There was a sister; there was a brother.

The brother's name was Gajulaj Mergen. The sister's name was Abak Nogon Agur, but here I'll call her by other names – the Sister, or the Girl, or the Hero in the Black Iron Armour.

The brother and the sister lived in a marvellous four-cornered house, and all around their marvellous four-cornered house was an expanse of fields and meadows and grazing pastures for their countless herds and flocks of goats and sheep and horses.

One day, the brother said to the sister, 'Today I feel like eating meat for dinner.'

The sister said, 'We have plenty of meat – sheep and goat and horse. What will you have?'

He said, 'Hmmm. I fancy the meat of a wild animal for dinner.'

And the sister said, 'Well if that's what you want, you must go hunting.'

He said, 'I will!'

He dressed himself in his hunting clothes, he went to the silver tethering post, and he called to his slender chestnut horse. His slender chestnut horse was listening for his call and came running to the silver tethering post.

Gajulaj Mergen said, 'Today I'm going hunting for game.'

The slender chestnut horse whinnied and offered advice in reply.

Gajulaj Mergen did not listen to the words of the horse. Nevertheless, the slender chestnut horse bowed his head for the halter.

They rode over the steppe, over plain and meadow, but Gajulaj Mergen saw no game. They came to the lowlands and found no game. They climbed through the rocky paths of the foothills and found no game, but at last they came to a high place that was charred by fire and ruined by conflict. And there was a seven-headed demon seated on a huge black horse.

The demon laughed seven loud laughs when it saw Gajulaj Mergen, and so did the black horse. Gajulaj Mergen raised his bow and reached for an arrow. But before he could place the arrow on the bowstring, the creature cried out with seven voices, 'What is that behind you? Is that your soul? Or is it your horse's soul?'

Gajulaj Mergen paused. He had never been asked such a question. He was perplexed and intrigued by the question. Also, he was unused to the tricks of demons. Wondering what was behind him – his own soul or his horse's soul – he looked behind.

And in that moment, the seven-headed demon leaped and devoured Gajulaj Mergen. Then the demon laughed loudly and wickedly and left.

Back in the four-cornered house, the sister was waiting. She heard the whinny of the slender chestnut horse at the tethering post. Out she went, and there at the tethering post, she found the horse, riderless.

She asked, 'Where is my brother?'

The horse told her the whole story.

Without a word, she put on her hunting gear, took up her

arrows and mounted the slender chestnut horse. They rode till they came to the devastated landscape.

There was the seven-headed demon. It smiled seven charming smiles. It raised and pointed a bony finger. It opened seven pairs of dry lips, but before it could speak, the sister spoke. In a clear voice, she said, 'Sir! I have a question. Is that your soul behind you, or is it your horse's soul?'

The seven-headed demon was unaccustomed to this sort of proactive questioning. It was unaccustomed to the tricks of girls. All seven pairs of eyes squinted. The seven heads looked at each other, puzzled and curious.

The demon turned all seven of its heads to see whose soul was behind it – its own soul or its horse's soul. And on that instant, the sister let fly seven arrows, one for each of the seven demon necks, and as the seventh arrow pierced the seventh neck, the demon fell to the ground with a crash.

The sister slid from the saddle, stooped beside the body of the demon, and with her dagger she slit open the belly of the demon.

Behind her, the horse whinnied, 'Not in its belly.'

So, she slit open the heart of the demon.

Behind her, the horse whinnied, 'Not in its heart.'

She turned to the horse and cried out, 'Where will I find the bones of my brother?'

And the horse said, 'In the thumb.'

'The thumb?'

'You'll find the bones of your brother in the thumb of the demon.'

So, she slit open the thumb of the dead demon and there she found the bones of her brother. She took them home.

When she arrived home, she tended to the horse and then to the bones. She washed the bones of her brother in the waters from seven streams. She laid the bones on strips of bark from seven birch forests and she wrapped the bones of her brother in silks of seven colours. Then she and the horse travelled to the holy mountain Angaj.

At the foot of the holy mountain Angaj, she knelt. She called out, 'Holy mountain Angaj! Receive the bones of my brother!'

At her words, there was a groan from the stone and a mouth in the mountain opened. She placed the bones within the heart of the holy mountain Angaj, and the mouth in the mountain closed around the bones of the brother.

And then she and the slender chestnut horse returned to her own house. She took off the hunting garb, dressed herself in her own clothes and she returned to hearth. There, she sat at the hearth and began to weep.

The mountains and the furnace.

Beside the flames of her own hearth, she said, 'What am I to do? My brother whom I loved is dead. My protector who was everything to me is gone. Who will look after me now? Who will be my guardian now? I am nothing now. I am no one now. I can achieve nothing alone. My brother was all to me. But he is dead, and not even God can bring back the dead to the world of the living.' She wept for a long time by the fire.

Outside, under the stars, the slender chestnut horse was waiting.

Now, here are some things that you need to know.

The first is that God's name is Eseg Malen, and he lives on the Mountain of Heaven.

You need to know that Eseg Malen is great and wise and powerful, but not even he is powerful enough to bring the dead back to life.

You need to know that Eseg Malen, Old Father God, has three beautiful swan daughters and their power is greater than his. The three swan daughters of God can do the thing that even God can't do.

Eseg Malen is very old and wise and all knowing. The three swan daughters of Eseg Malen are very young and not always wise at all, but they are immeasurably powerful. Not even Eseg Malen has the power to bring the dead to this world, but the daughters of God can bring the dead back – and they will do it – but only at the request of a lover, a suitor.

'Well,' said the sister by the fire, 'The daughters of God will bring back the dead for a suitor. I must have my brother back and so I must become a suitor. I must win the daughters of God as my wives. And if there is deception in this and they are angry at this deception, let the anger fall on my head – but I must have my brother back.'

The sister walked back through the corridors of the four-cornered house to her brother's chamber and took down his black iron armour. She dressed herself in the black iron armour and looked into the mirror and saw, looking back at her, one who was every inch the Hero in the Black Iron Armour.

She went to the silver tethering post and called to the slender chestnut horse, and he came at her call. She said, 'I must travel to the Mountain of God.'

The horse spoke, and when he spoke, she listened.

The horse said, 'The way will be long.'

She said, 'So be it.'

'The way will be arduous.'

She said, 'So be it.'

'The way will be painful.'

She said, 'So be it.'

'So be it,' said the horse. 'And once you have chosen the path, all you have to do is sit strong and steady in the saddle and keep going. Can you do that?'

'I can.'

And they began the journey.

For a long time and for a short time they travelled, and the girl sat strong and steady in the saddle. They came at last to a three-cornered crossroad.

There was an old woman. The old woman crouched, fanning a small fire. On a tripod above the fire simmered an iron pot, full of hot tea. The old woman beamed up at the girl. She said, 'Oh, my dear! You do look tired.'

And suddenly, the girl did feel terribly tired.

'You must be so thirsty.'

And suddenly the girl did feel terribly thirsty.

The old woman said, 'I've just brewed up this lovely tea, dear. Why don't you slip down here, taste a sip of my tea and relax for a bit by the fire. You look so sad. Tell me your troubles.'

It was very tempting. The girl slid down from her saddle, but as her feet touched the earth, she heard the voice of the

horse saying, 'Don't taste that tea. If you taste that tea, all
your resolve and all your endeavour is as nothing. Rather,
you should throw the tea in the old woman's fire.'

The girl heard the words of her horse. It seemed such a
rude thing to do. The old woman held up the cup and the
girl took it. But she did not taste it. Instead, she threw it in
the old woman's fire. And the tea and the old woman were
gone on the instant.

But the fire ... that was leaping higher – high as the sky.
The fire was roaring. It was the fire that burns between this
world and the otherworld. Beyond the fire is the Mountain of
Heaven – the mountain of Eseg Malen – of Old Father God.

The horse spoke and the girl was listening. He said, 'Now
we must make a great leap through the fire between earth
and heaven, and the fire will burn. Do you remember your
resolve? Can you stay strong and steady in the saddle?'

And the girl said she could.

The horse reared up and galloped and took a great leap
through the flaming furnace. She felt the fire through the black
iron armour, and all the time the voice of the horse was calling.
'Are you steady in the saddle? Are you strong in the saddle?'

And she called back, 'Yes, steady and strong!'

And again, he was calling, 'Steady and strong?'

And she called back, 'Yes!'

But on the third time he called, 'Steady and strong?', she
called back, 'I am in the saddle, but I am terribly burned.'

And he said, 'We are through the fire. And that you are in
the saddle at all is to be considered a great success.'

The horse was standing in the foothills of the Mountain
of Heaven and the fire was roaring behind them. The girl
slid from the saddle and tore off the armour.

The horse said, 'What do you see?'

'Nothing. I am blinded by the fire.'

The horse said, 'What do you hear?'

'I hear the tinkling of a little stream nearby.'

The horse said, 'That is the stream that flows down the Mountain of Heaven and into the abyss between our worlds. It is the water of life. That is the sound to follow.'

And the girl moved towards the sound of the tinkling stream. Her fingers felt the cool water and she washed herself in it and drank of it and was restored.

She saw that she sat beside a bright stream, meandering down the Mountain of Heaven and disappearing into mist and flame below. It was a silver thread that ran between rock and moss from a high peak far above. Her sight was restored and was clearer than before and it seemed that the singing of the stream and the wind over the rocks was clearer and sharper, and all her senses were clearer and sharper after the bathing and the drinking.

She bathed the horse's wounds and gave him water, and the horse too was better and stronger and more beautiful than before. Then she filled a bottle from the stream of the water of life.

She put the bottle of the water of life into the horse's saddlebag, and they rode on upward. They followed the mountain path upward until they came to a place where the path forked. With her new sharp ears, she heard a sound but could see nothing. She said, 'I hear a groan.'

The horse said, 'Follow the sound.'

And lying beside the fork in the path was a man, where she'd not seen a man before. This man had been a warrior or a hero, but he was a hero no more. His eyes were hollow, his lips were cracked and his ribs stuck out. He was a hero who had seen better days. He was a hero close to death. The sister slid down and sat beside him. She said, 'Hero, what happened?'

He said, 'I drank the old woman's tea and now I will never reach my goal or my journey's end.'

She said, 'We'll see about that.'

She took the bottle from the horse's saddlebag and gave him a drop to drink. His eyes brightened. His chest filled out. He leapt to his feet. He cried, 'You've restored me, and as you have helped me, so I will help you! I am the Hero of Heaven, and I will help you when you need. Just call on me.' And he was gone.

They followed the stony path of the mountain upward and the sounds were the clatter and scrape of hooves, until they came to a place where the path forked. She heard a sound. She said, 'I hear a whimper, but I see nothing.'

'Then you must follow the sound.'

And lying there was a yellow dog, where she'd seen no dog before. He was a dog who'd seen better days. His eyes were hollow, his ribs stuck out and his skin was mangey. This was a dog close to death.

The girl sat by his side and said, 'What happened? Did you drink the tea?'

'Yes. I drank the old woman's tea and now I will never achieve my goals or reach my journey's end.'

But she gave him a drop to drink from the bottle and he leapt up, barking loudly, and swore he would be her friend to the end. 'I am the Hound of Heaven! I will help you if you need me. Just call on me and I will bring help when you need help.' And he was gone.

And now they were very far up on the Mountain of Heaven. Looking into the mist above, she saw a plateau and there was a little yurt, and at the tethering post outside, two horses were tied – a white and a red. The girl tethered the slender chestnut horse, ducked her head to enter the house on the Mountain of Heaven, and she found herself within a cosy room.

There was a fire. In the shadows beyond the fire, an old woman was sitting knitting. There was a cloth laden with good food. There were two strong heroes sitting eating. One was dressed in red and the other in white. And standing before the fire, all dressed in green silk, was Eseg Malen, Old Father God himself. He was holding wide his arms. He said, 'Oh, very good indeed! Here he is. Here is the third suitor! Now all can begin.'

And then he asked, 'Who are you?

And the girl said, 'I am Gajulaj Mergen, the Hero of the Black Iron Armour.'

'Very good,' said Old Father God. 'Now we have three suitors, the White, the Red and the Black. So, we can begin the courting.'

He gave a call, and the door flew open and into the yurt came gliding the three beautiful swan daughters of God – so beautiful that I'll not try to describe them!

It was a great evening of entertainment that followed. They were all talking at once. But through the evening of entertainment, if the eldest daughter was laughing, the youngest was crying, and if the youngest was laughing, the eldest was crying, and through it all, the middle daughter was always watching.

At the end of the evening, Eseg Malen said, 'You know the rules. There are three suitors, but only one of you will win all three of my daughters. They come as a set. They cannot be parted. We will begin tomorrow. Agreed?' He looked into the shadows beyond the fire, where the old wise woman was still sitting knitting. She nodded.

Next day, they were all up with the dawn. The sky was clearest blue. Eagles were circling above the Mountain of Heaven. The assembled courtiers of Old Father God were beautiful and silent.

Eseg Malen spoke, 'Today my three swan daughters will choose their husband.' Then he looked at the heroes. 'Of course, you Heroes will have to pass tests and trials to gauge your usefulness as suitors.'

He looked at his daughters indulgently. 'What will the test be, daughters?'

And all the daughters spoke at once and the middle one was saying loudly, 'Let us hear their stories.'

But the eldest was saying, 'Let them run a race.'

And the youngest was saying loudest of all, 'Wrestling!'

'Well, then,' said Old Father God. 'Wrestling it will be.'

So, the red and the white heroes started doing push-ups and lifting weights and swinging clubs, but our hero turned to talk to her horse. She said, 'What am I to do? I can't fight!'

The horse said, 'You fought the seven-headed demon and defeated him.'

She said, 'True. But that was a trick. No one could call me strong.'

'Well,' said the horse, 'That's your strength. Your strength is trickery, so it's trickery you must use. Call on the help of your friends.'

She called on the Hero of Heaven and when he came, no one saw him come but her.

When the red and the white heroes entered the wrestling ring and fell to the floor with cries and slaps and thumps, and everyone heard the crunch of bones, and the referee counted them out, and they were carried out of the hall helpless, everyone thought it was the Hero in the Black Iron Armour who had done it. No one saw the Hero of Heaven slip out of the hall, and everyone said they'd never seen a fight better fought.

Then the three swan daughters stepped forward to attend the wounded heroes. They each brought out a red handkerchief. The first girl flicked her handkerchief and the broken bones of the heroes mended with a snap. The second flicked her handkerchief and their wounds healed. The third flicked her handkerchief and the wounded heroes breathed deep and healthy once more.

And Eseg Malen, Old Father God, drew the sister in her black iron armour to him in a warm embrace. He called out, 'We have a clear winner! The Hero of the Black Iron Armour has won the match. I therefore give my daughters to the Hero of the Black Iron Armour.'

There was a little cough from the shadows, and the old wise woman knitting there, beyond the fire, said, 'You can do that, Father God, and it is within your right, but I tell you now, that if you give your three swan daughters to the Hero of the Black Iron Armour, you will be giving your daughters to a woman.'

Old Father God dropped his embrace and looked hard at the sister, then at the old wise woman. 'No!' He said, 'Not possible! And yet there is no point keeping wisdom at your fireside and not listening to her. Listen and I'll tell you why.'

Everyone sat down and Eseg Malen began a story. 'At the very beginning of time, when I created man and woman, and they roamed free and I watched over them, I was delighted! I gathered all the wisdom there was, broke all that wisdom into thirteen parts and I dropped it – I let it drift on the wind down to Earth. It so happened that First Woman was out in the field gleaning, and First Man was taking a nap under a tree. One part of all my wisdom drifted down and straight into the open mouth of First Man. The other twelve parts fell into the field and First Woman gathered all of them up and kept them safe. She has got them out and used them ever since, whenever they were needed. Of all the wisdom in the world, woman has twelve parts of the thirteen parts of wisdom. So, of course, that's why I've got an old wise woman to advise me.'

'So we'd better have another test. Daughters, what shall it be?'

The middle daughter said, 'Let's hear their stories!'

But the eldest was shouting, 'Race!'

'Then a race it will be,' said Old Father God.

The red and the white heroes ran out to brush their horses, polish their saddles and clean their tack. But our hero was talking to her horse.

She said, 'What am I to do?'

The horse said, 'You have ridden across the world, through the fire between the worlds and up the mountain of god!'

She said, 'True, we've travelled far, but no one could call us fast.'

The horse said, 'What matters in a race is not that you're fast, but that you're first. Call on the help of your friends.'

So, she called on the Hound of Heaven, and he came. And when the red and the white horses skittered and reared, no one saw the hound as he was nipping and biting at their hocks. The chestnut horse crossed the line easily, and everyone said they'd never seen a race better run.

At the finishing line, Old Father God embraced the girl. He said, 'Here is the Hero in the Black Iron Armour, and he has won my three swan daughters fair and square. He was first.'

But again, there was a little cough.

The old woman said, 'You can give your three swan daughters to the Hero in the Black Iron Armour if you like, but you will be giving your daughters to a woman.'

Eseg Malen let loose his embrace. He gave the girl a fond look. He turned to the old wise woman, who sat knitting. He walked over to her and sat down. 'Old woman,' he said, 'I dropped thirteen pieces of wisdom to the world and woman has twelve of those pieces of wisdom and man has one.'

Then he took a cushion and he said, 'Old woman, I know you will always tell me the truth.' He put the cushion on the floor and sat beside her at the fire. He said, 'Old wise woman, let me tell you a story.

'A man travelled in search of the truth. In the end, he found the truth very far away and high up in a little mountain cave. The truth was very old and bony and wrinkly. She had no hair and only one tooth. But when she spoke to him, he recognised her voice. It was so clear and beautiful. He recognised her for what she was: the truth.

'He lived with her, and he studied with her for a long time.

'At last, he said, "I think it's time for me to go home and tell the world what I've learned from you."

'And she said, "I think so, too."

'As he left, he said, "Mistress Truth, you've taught me well. Tell me what to say about you when I return to the world of humans."

'At that, she laughed a creaky laugh and smiled a toothless smile and said, "Tell them I am young and beautiful."'

Eseg Malen said, 'Old woman, beneath every wise truth, there is a deeper and a wiser truth.' Then he rose and turned and spoke to everyone. 'I give my three swan daughters to Gajulaj Mergen, the Hero of the Black Iron Armour, to be their husband.'

And there was a big wedding.

As the wedding preparations were under way, the eldest daughter of God came to the sister and said, 'Betrothed, now we are to be married, take off your black iron armour and put on this smart satin suit.'

But the sister said, 'I have sworn not to take off my black iron armour until I return home.'

After the wedding, there was a big party planned. The youngest daughter of God said, 'Husband, take off that black iron armour. Put on this light silk dancing suit.'

But the sister said, 'I have sworn not to take off my black iron armour until I return home.'

When the feasting was over and the guests were going home, the middle daughter came. She said, 'Now we are married, husband, take off the black iron armour.'

But the sister said, 'I have sworn not to take off my black iron armour until I return home.'

The next day, Old Father God embraced the sister. He said, 'Son-in-law, I will build you a grand four-cornered house, right next to my little yurt, here on the Mountain of Heaven.'

But the sister said, 'I have a house and a hearth of my own, and I must return there.'

'Very good,' said Old Father God. 'That's as it should be.' Then he offered his children a wedding present. 'What would you like?'

The eldest daughter said, 'Gold', and the youngest said, 'Jewels'.

But the middle daughter was quicker this time, and she said, 'Let our marriage gift be the silver ladle that hangs behind the door of the kitchen of heaven.'

'Oh, very good,' said Old Father God. 'Because that's the thing of most value on the Mountain of Heaven, and indeed in all the world. Anyone who has the silver ladle will never know need, hunger, or thirst.'

The eldest and the youngest daughters reached for it, but the middle one already had it in her hand, and she said, 'Here is our marriage gift.'

On their way down the mountain, the family stopped to camp. While the husband lit the fire and ladled the supper from the silver ladle, the daughters of God got to gossiping about their husband.

The eldest daughter said, 'Our husband is affable and amenable.'

The youngest said, 'Yes. He's a good listener and not at all arrogant.'

The middle daughter said, 'He is smooth-skinned and slim. These are not the qualities of a man. Could the old woman be right? Has our father married us to a woman?'

'Oh no! Do you think so?'

'We need a test. Let's throw a snake on him. If he screams

and recoils, it's a woman. If he brushes it off and drives it away, it's a man.'

'No. Let's throw an ember from the fire. If he cries out and runs about, it's a woman. If he brushes the ember aside without a second glance, it's a man.'

They waited till their husband slept. They took an ember from the fire. They threw it onto the breast of the sleeping girl, who woke with a start, brushed it off without a second glance, turned over and slept again.

Then they searched in the brushwood for a snake. They threw it onto the chest of the sleeping girl. She woke, brushed off the snake, took a stick and drove it into the under-growth. Then returning to the fire, she lay down and slept again.

The eldest daughter of God said, 'Definitely a man.'

'Yes,' said the youngest. 'Definitely a man.'

They rose the next morning and reached the bottom of the mountain. When they faced the flames between the Mountain of Heaven and the plains of Earth, the eldest daughter of God took out her handkerchief. She flicked it, and the fire disappeared.

The youngest daughter of God took out her handkerchief. She flicked it, and there was a bridge between the Mountain of Heaven and Earth.

They all rode across, and as they reached the other side, the middle daughter of Old Father Eseg Malen shook her handkerchief, and the bridge was gone and the flames leapt up once more.

Now our hero turned to the daughters of God and said, 'I will ride ahead to prepare my house for you. I will leave signs for you. Where the path leads left, I will leave a sign. Where the path leads right, I will leave a sign.' And she left the three swan daughters of God to ride at leisure, while she rode on ahead.

Once she was home, she rode the horse to the holy mountain Angaj. She called out, 'Holy mountain Angaj! Give up the bones of my brother.'

There was a groan in the stone, and a mouth in the mountain opened. She took out the bones of her brother.

She returned to the four-cornered house. She carried the bones of her brother through the halls and corridors and came to the hearth. She lit the fire and unbundled her burden. Beside the flames of the fire in their four-cornered house, she set out the bones of her brother. She laid out his bones, all in order from the skull to the toes. She laid the Black Iron Armour beside the bones and put on her own clothes.

Then she went to tend to the slender chestnut horse, which waited at the tethering post.

When the horse was fed and watered, she began to sing and weave into the mane of the horse the story of all that had happened. She worked quickly, but not quickly enough. As she wove the last word into the mane of the horse, she heard the thud of hooves, and the three daughters of God appeared in the distance.

She wove the last word into the mane.

She took the silver ladle from her side, raised it, and turned herself into a little hare, which leapt away from the tethering post and out across the steppe. The silver ladle clattered to the ground.

The daughters of God called out, 'Who's that beside our husband's horse?'

But when they arrived by the tethering post, there was no one.

The three swan daughters of God dismounted from their horses at the tethering post, and the eldest and the youngest entered the house. But the middle girl stopped beside the tethering post and picked up the silver ladle. Then she began to stroke the mane of the slender chestnut horse.

The eldest and the youngest were walking through the halls of the house calling out, 'Gajulaj Mergen! Husband! We have come! We are here! Welcome your wives!' But the only sound was the echo of their own voices. They came at last to the hearth and saw no welcome, but only the bones lying there.

They were very annoyed. 'What is this? The daughters of God come to meet their bridegroom and find no welcome, but only the echoes of their own voices and the bones of a man lying by the fire. Let's go home!'

Then their sister joined them. She said, 'Wait. I have read the story written in the mane of the horse. These are the bones of a brother, and the sister runs as a hare on the mountain.'

The eldest and the youngest were outraged. 'The old woman was right. The wicked girl has deceived us. She has cheated us.'

They wanted to go home, but the middle sister said, 'No. It's true that we have been summoned here by trickery. But here we are. We are summoned by tricks to this world of women and men. Before we leave this world, we must do what is in our power to do. Why would we not? Come on now. Do.'

And it was agreed.

They stood together. And the eldest spat on the bones of Gajulaj Mergen. She flicked her red handkerchief and jumped over the bones beside the fire. As she did, there was a clicking and a crackle, and the bones knit back together.

Then the youngest spat on the knitted bones and she flicked her red handkerchief and jumped over the fire. As she did, muscle slithered back over bone, skin and hair formed, and Gajulaj Mergen, the hero of the Black Iron Armour, lay naked beside the fire. All the sisters tilted their heads and, against their own will, each murmured appreciatively.

Then the middle daughter of God spat, and she flicked her red handkerchief and she jumped. As she did, the breath entered the chest of the hero and it rose and fell again. His cheeks flushed and his fingers and his toes twitched, and the hero sat up, all black haired and beautiful. He looked around, and Gajulaj Mergen saw the three daughters of God, who were all smiling down at him.

He jumped up and said, 'Where is my sister?' He ran to the silver tethering post and he looked around. There was no one there but the horse. He asked, 'Where is my sister?'

The horse told him the whole story and Gajulaj Mergen heard every word. Gajulaj Mergen said, 'We must ride and find her!'

But the horse said, 'I have ridden to the Mountain of the Seven-Headed Demon twice. I have ridden to the Holy Mountain Angaj twice. I have ridden to the Mountain of Heaven and back, and now I am very tired. Within the house, the three daughters of God are awaiting the attentions of their husband. Let us wait a week and then ride out.'

And for the second time, Gajulaj Mergen listened to the words of his horse. He returned to his hearth, where the three swan daughters of God were waiting for him. He paid suitable attention to the daughters of God and didn't put on his black iron armour at all.

But at the end of that time, he returned to the horse and then they rode out onto the steppe, and they searched for a long time, until at last they found that little hare and the brother caught her. She wriggled and she kicked, but he did not let her go, until, at last, she returned to her true form.

And when the sister stood before the brother, she spoke. 'I have killed the seven-headed demon for you. I have ridden to the Mountain of Heaven for you. I have deceived the daughters of God for you.'

And he said, 'I know. I was asleep. Now I am awake. I was deaf. Now I can hear. I was dead. Now I am alive. Thank you. Let's go home.'

She was afraid of the anger of the daughters of God. But to know everything is to forgive everything. They understood. They knew the story.

Now listen to the words which were spoken by the daughters of God: 'We were married to the sister, but our husband is the brother. Our husband is the brother, so we have him at our side. But we were married to the sister, and it is to her we return our wedding gift.'

They gave her the silver ladle from behind the door of God's kitchen, and she tied it at her waist. Then she bade them goodbye, and she stepped out with the Ladle of Plenty, into the world. If ever you come to a place that has enough, you'll know she's not long been through.

She's travelling still, with the silver ladle from the Kitchen of Heaven. She'll keep on travelling until the whole wide world has enough. And her name is Abak Nogon Agur.

8

Inanna's Descent to the Underworld

Inanna was Queen of Earth and Heaven. But she was not Queen of the Underworld. That honour belonged to the goddess Ereshkigal. Her realm was the Underworld, the Kingdom of the Dead. No one went there out of choice, for no one who went there ever returned.

Yet Inanna decided to go.

Was it, as she said, to attend the funeral rites for Ereshkigal's husband? Or was it to challenge Ereshkigal's authority?

She made her preparations with care.

She dressed herself in the seven symbols of her power. She did not intend to go there naked, like a corpse, but adorned, like a queen.

On her head, she placed her crown, the shugurra.

About her neck, she set a strand of lapis lazuli.

Across her shoulder, she draped a long string of lapis beads.

She strapped her golden breastplate about her chest.

She slipped bracelets of gold around her wrists.

She took her measuring rod and line in her hands.

She wrapped her body in her royal robe, the pala garment.

When she was ready, she called her dear companion, Ninshubur. 'My friend, I am about to set out on the path to the place from which no one has ever returned.

'Walk with me.

She dressed herself in her symbols of power.

'Walk with me until we come to the place from which each one must go on alone. Wait for me there, until I return.'

Ninshubur agreed. Why would she not? She was a good friend.

Inanna had more to say, more to ask. 'Wait there for three days and three nights. If, after three days and nights, I have not returned, you will know that I need your help. You must be my voice when I cannot speak. You must ask the gods to help me.

'Will you do this for me, Ninshubur?'

Ninshubur agreed. Why would she not? She was Inanna's heart-companion.

They set their feet on the path from which no one has ever returned. They walked together until they came to the place from which each one must go on alone. There, Inanna stopped. She said, 'Wait for me here, Ninshubur. Do not forget what you have promised.'

Ninshubur pressed Inanna's hands and sat down at the roadside.

Without a backward glance, Inanna went on alone. She walked until she came to the great gate of the Underworld. She knocked loudly on the gate, crying out, 'Gatekeeper, open the gate! I am Inanna, and I would enter.'

Neti, the Gatekeeper of the Underworld, answered from behind the great gates. 'If you are truly Inanna, Queen of Earth and Heaven, why has your heart brought you on the path from which no one has ever returned?'

Inanna replied, 'Because of my sister, Ereshkigal. Her husband has died. I have come to witness the funeral rites. Open the gate. Let it be done.'

Neti did not know what to do. No one had ever come to his gates of their own free will before. He called out, 'Wait there, Inanna, I will tell my Queen what you have said.'

Down he went; down to the Great Hall of Ereshkigal's dark palace. His queen sat on her grim stone throne. He bowed low before her. 'My Lady,' he said, 'A woman waits at your gates. She is as tall as the sky, as broad as the horizon, as strong as the city walls. She is wearing the symbols of power. On her head she wears a crown. Around her neck are chains of lapis beads, both short and long. She wears a golden breastplate and golden bracelets. She carries a measuring rod and line. She is dressed in a royal robe, a pala garment.'

When she had heard all this, Ereshkigal chewed her lip. She considered the facts. She planned her response. She said, 'Let her enter, Neti. But make sure she enters naked and bowed low, as do all who enter here.

'Lock the seven gates of the Underworld against her.

'Bolt the seven doors of the Underworld against her.

'As she comes to each gate, take one of her symbols of power from her.

'Let her enter my realm naked and humbled, as do all who enter here.'

Neti, the gatekeeper, heard the words of his queen. He listened to her commands. He obeyed them.

He locked the seven gates of the Underworld. He bolted the seven doors of the Underworld.

He opened the first gate of the Underworld a crack, saying, 'Come, Inanna, enter.'

As Inanna went through the gate, the crown was snatched from her head. She said, 'What is this?'

Many voices replied, saying, 'Be silent, Inanna. The ways of the Underworld are perfect. They may not be questioned.'

She was shaken, but she went on.

Neti opened the second gate of the Underworld a crack, saying, 'Come, Inanna, enter.'

As Inanna went through the gate, the lapis necklace was pulled from her neck. She said, 'What is this?'

They said, 'Be silent, Inanna. The ways of the Underworld are perfect. They may not be questioned.'

She was troubled, but she went on.

She came to the third gate of the Underworld. Neti opened it a little, saying, 'Come, Inanna, enter.'

As Inanna went through the gate, the long chain of lapis was taken from her. She said, 'What is this?'

They said, 'Be silent, Inanna. The ways of the Underworld are perfect. They may not be questioned.'

And so it went on.

At the fourth gate they took her golden breastplate.

At the fifth, her golden bracelets.

At the sixth, they took her measuring rod and line.

At the seventh, her royal robe was torn from her body.

Each time she cried out, 'What is this?' Each time they said, 'Be silent, Inanna. The ways of the Underworld are perfect. They may not be questioned.'

When she entered the Great Hall of the Underworld, she was naked and bowed low, as were all who entered there.

Ereshkigal was sitting on her great stone throne. She watched Inanna enter. She fixed upon Inanna the eye of wrath. She fixed upon her the eye of guilt. She stretched out her hand and spoke a word of power.

Inanna was struck down. She was changed to a corpse, a piece of rotting meat, which they hung from a hook on the wall.

For three days and three nights, it hung there.

For three days and three nights, Ninshubur waited at the appointed place.

When, after three days and nights, Inanna had not returned, Ninshubur tore at her face, at her arms and her thighs. She rubbed ash into her hair and dressed herself in a mourning garment. She cried out for Inanna in the market place. She beat the drum for Inanna in the gathering place. She went to the temples of the gods to ask for their help.

She entered the great hall of the Underworld.

When she entered the temple of the god Enlil, she bowed before the altar. She lifted her hands in prayer. She cried out, 'O, Father Enlil, do not let the Lady Inanna be lost in the Underworld!'

Father Enlil heard the words of Ninshubur, but he did not listen to them. He simply said, 'The ways of the Underworld are perfect. They may not be questioned. Who, having once gone down to that place, would expect to come back again?' He would not help her.

Ninshubur went on. She came to the temple of the god An. When she entered An's temple, she bowed before the altar. She lifted her hands in prayer. Once again she prayed, 'O, Father An, do not let the Lady Inanna be lost in the Underworld.'

Father An heard the words of Ninshubur, but he did not listen to them. He too said, 'The ways of the Underworld are perfect. They may not be questioned. Who, having once gone down to that place, would expect to come back again?' He would not help her.

Ninshubur went on. She came to the temple of the god of wisdom, Enki, the all-seeing, all-knowing one. She entered Enki's temple, the Abzu, beside the deep, sweet water. A third time, she bowed before an altar. A third time she prayed, 'O, Father Enki, do not let the Lady Inanna be lost in the Underworld.

'Do not let your bright silver be covered by the dust of the Underworld.

'Do not let your fragrant box wood be chopped into pieces for the woodworker.

'Do not let your precious lapis be broken into fragments for the stone worker.

'Do not let the Lady Inanna be lost in the Underworld.'

Enki, all-seeing, all-knowing, heard Ninshubur's words. He listened to her. He said, 'What has happened to the Lady Inanna? I am troubled. I am grieved. I will help her.'

Father Enki stretched out his left arm. From under the nail of the middle finger of his left hand, he scraped out dust. From it, he made a creature neither male nor female: a kurgarra.

Then he stretched out his right arm. From under the nail of the middle finger of his right hand, he scraped out more dust. From it, he made a creature neither female nor male: a galatur.

To the kurgarra he gave the water of life.

To the galatur he gave the food of life.

He spoke to these creatures. He said, 'Make yourselves as small as flies. Slip through the cracks in the seven gates of the Underworld. Slide through the bolts of the seven gates of the Underworld, until you reach the Great Hall. There you will see Ereshkigal moaning and groaning, as if she were about to give birth.

'When she sighs, 'Oh, my heart', you must sigh, 'Oh, your heart'.

'When she cries, 'Oh, my liver!', you must cry, 'Oh, your liver!'

'When she hears you sighing and crying, moaning and groaning for her, she will be moved by your empathy. She will offer you a gift.

'She will offer you the grain gift, the fields ready for harvest.

'Do not accept it.

'She will offer you the water gift, the river in spate.

'Do not accept it.

'Ask her only for the corpse that hangs from a hook on the wall. When it is taken down and given to you, sprinkle it with the water of life. Sprinkle it with the food of life. Inanna will arise. Send Inanna back from the Underworld.'

The kurgarra and the galatur obeyed Enki. They made themselves as small as flies. They slipped through the gates and slid through the bolts, until they reached Ereshkigal's Great Hall.

There they found Ereshkigal. She was sighing and crying, moaning and groaning. No clothes covered her body. Her breasts were bare. Her hair swirled around her head like leeks.

She sighed, 'Oh, my heart.' They sighed, 'Oh, your heart.'

She cried, 'Oh, my liver!' They cried, 'Oh, your liver!'

She moaned, 'Oh, my inside.' They moaned, 'Oh, your inside.'

She groaned, 'Oh, my outside.' They groaned, 'Oh, your outside.'

She stopped sighing, crying, moaning and groaning. She looked at them. She said, 'Who are you? If you are gods, I will worship you. If you are mortal, I will give you a gift. I will give you the grain gift, the fields ready for harvest.'

They said, 'We do not want it.'

She said, 'I will give you the water gift, the river in spate.'

They said, 'We do not want it.'

She said, 'What *is* it that you want?'

They said, 'We ask only for the corpse that hangs from a hook on the wall.'

She said, 'That is the corpse of Inanna.'

They said, 'We know.'

The corpse was taken down and given to them. The kurgarra sprinkled the corpse with the water of life. The galatur added the food of life.

Inanna was restored. She turned to leave the Underworld, but the galla, the demons of the Underworld, surrounded her. They cried out, 'The ways of the Underworld are perfect! They may not be questioned. Who, having once come down to this place, can expect to go back again?'

Inanna answered, 'I do, and I will.'

The galla spoke again, 'If Inanna would return from the Underworld, she must send another in her place. The bargain with death cannot be broken.'

Inanna looked around her, at the demons, at the Great

Hall, at its Queen. Then, without another word, she left. As she climbed the long stairway, through the seven gates and the seven doors, the galla surrounded Inanna. They could not stop her, but they would not leave her. They walked with Inanna until she came to the place where she had parted from Ninshubur.

Ninshubur, ash in her hair, her face gashed and torn, her body wrapped in a mourning garment, was waiting at the appointed place. When she saw Inanna returning, she flung herself into the dust at Inanna's feet.

The galla said, 'Walk on, Inanna. We will take Ninshubur in your place.'

But Inanna said, 'No! Ninshubur is my heart's companion. She is my friend. She waited here for me. She cried out my name in the houses of the gods. Because of her I am restored. I will never give Ninshubur to you!'

'Very well,' said the galla. 'Walk on, Inanna. We will go further with you.'

Inanna walked on until she came to the city of her son, Shara. Shara, ash in his hair, his face gashed and torn, was dressed in a mourning garment. When he saw Inanna returning, he flung himself into the dust at her feet.

The galla said, 'Walk on, Inanna. We will take Shara in your place.'

But Inanna said, 'No! Shara cuts my nails and combs my hair. He is my dear son. I will never give Shara to you!'

'Very well,' said the galla. 'Walk on, Inanna. We will go further with you.'

Inanna went on until she came to the city of her second son, Lulal. Lulal, ash in his hair, his face gashed and torn, was dressed in a mourning garment. When he saw Inanna returning, he flung himself into the dust at her feet.

The galla said, 'Walk on, Inanna. We will take Lulal in your place.'

But Inanna said, 'No! Lulal is a leader. He is my right arm. He is my dear son. I will never give Lulal to you!'

'Very well,' said the galla. 'Walk on, Inanna. We will go further with you.'

Inanna went on until she came to the city of her husband, Dumuzi. Dumuzi was dressed in gleaming garments. He wore the shugurra crown on his head. He was seated on a shining throne. When he saw Inanna returning, he did not move.

Inanna looked long at Dumuzi. She fixed upon him the eye of wrath. She fixed upon him the eye of guilt. She stretched out her hand and cried out, 'Take him! Take Dumuzi in my place!'

The galla surrounded Dumuzi. They dragged him away.

Inanna said, 'The ways of the Underworld are perfect. They may not be questioned.' She turned away and went into her city.

The people of the city wept for Dumuzi.

Dumuzi's mother wept for her son.

His sister Geshtinanna wept for her brother. She cried out, 'Who is my brother? You are he. Who is your sister? I am she. This world held both you and me. This is the same world we both did see. I would find my brother. I would share his fate.' She came weeping to Inanna.

Her tears moved Inanna. Inanna spoke, 'He shall go to the Underworld, but for half the year only. Because you have asked it, you will share his fate. On the day that Dumuzi comes up from the Underworld, Geshtinanna, on that day you will go down. On the day that you come up, on that day he will go down.'

And so it began.

The turning of the seasons.

Turning then, turning still.

VIEWS OF THE AFTERLIFE: ANCIENT SUMER

Here are two more stories from Mesopotamia. These stories, and the one you have just read, overlap chronologically. Because they operate in 'story time', not real time, the passing of time is not consistent between them. But between them they offer a window into this extremely ancient culture.

We are aware that we have weighted this collection rather heavily towards Sumerian stories. This is not because we feel they are core texts on death and dying. It is because this culture and its stories have been such a large part of our storytelling lives, from the middle of the 1990s onwards. This is due to the ground-breaking work of our friend, the storyteller and author, Fran Hazelton.

Fran's interest in the culture of Mesopotamia led her to create a storytelling company, Zipang, dedicated to performing Mesopotamian material. She then founded a charity, the Enheduanna Society, the aim of which is to popularise the literature of Ancient Iraq through the art of oral storytelling. We are both grateful to her for the learning and opportunities that have opened to us because of her vision.

The Sumerian view of the 'Ever After' is not a very encouraging one, either for us now or, surely, for them then. Their dead exist in a grey, cheerless afterlife and rely on their descendants for sustenance, as Enkidu relates in the first story below. Woe betide you if no one is making offerings for you. And there is also the dark description of the dead existing in the trauma of the manner of their death.

June writes:

My memories of my brother were coloured by the manner of his death.

I was clearing out my family home. A burst pipe flooded the house. We had to strip away the wallpaper. On the plaster underneath there was childish crayon writing. 'June loves Robbie'. I had to throw most things away. But some papers were left and amongst them, I found old letters of condolence to my parents, from Robbie's friends. They described him as a much loved friend who was a competent and talented adult. He was not the damaged child I had held in my heart after his death. After 20 years he was restored to me as the brother I loved.

In the second story here, taken from the *Epic of Gilgamesh*, we can see that Gilgamesh's fear of death, sparked by the irretrievable loss of his beloved friend Enkidu, must also spring from his culture's understanding of 'what comes after'. He sets out on a quest for eternal life; a quest that is ultimately unsuccessful. Humans are born to die; this is our fate, and nothing can change it.

Yet the words of Siduri, the wise woman, remind us how to experience the blessing that lies hidden in the curse of a limited lifespan: take comfort in all that life brings to you, and live it to the full.

9

ENKIDU

In the first days, in the very first days, in the first nights, in the very first nights, in those ancient days, a little Huluppu tree was growing by the side of the River Euphrates. One night, a terrible storm ripped the little Huluppu tree up by the roots and washed it downriver.

The next morning, the young girl, Inanna, was walking by the swollen river. She saw the little tree caught in the reeds by the river, waded in and fished it out. She took it back to her garden, planted it, stamped down the earth with her foot and spoke, 'As I grow to my full strength, so shall this little tree grow. In time it will give me the wood I need for my shining throne and my shining bed.'

Time passed and she tended the tree. She watered and she weeded around it. As she grew, so did the tree. At last, it was strong and tall, and Inanna spoke. 'Now I shall have my shining throne and my shining bed!'

But when she approached the tree, she saw that a snake had made its home in the roots of the tree and the Anzu bird had made its nest in the branches of the tree. When she looked within its trunk, she saw the dark maid, Lilith, grinning and winking and laughing at her.

In distress, she called on the help of her brother, Utu, the sun god. 'Oh Utu! I pulled the little tree from the waters of the River Euphrates. I have cared for it, so that in time it will provide me with my shining bed and my shining throne! Now in its roots there's a snake, in its branches there's the Anzu bird and within its trunk, the dark maid, Lilith!'

Her brother Utu was no help.

The young King Gilgamesh came striding by. 'Sister! Why so sad?'

'The tree! The snake! The Anzu bird! The dark maid! My bed! My throne!'

Young King Gilgamesh strapped on his belt and took his axe.

He struck once and the snake hissed and slithered away.

He struck a second time and the Anzu bird flew.

He struck a third time and, with a screech, Lilith retreated to the desert lands.

Gilgamesh felled the tree, stripped the branches and the trunk and laid them before the young Inanna. Gladly, she took them for her shining bed and her shining throne.

She was grateful and left him a gift: a little of the wood, some of the roots and branches of the Huluppu tree. Delighted, Gilgamesh took them to the woodworker. When he returned the next day, the woodworker had made for his king something wonderful and new. He had made an Ekidmar and an Elag.

An Ekidmar and an Elag. What could they be? A sceptre and an orb for a king?

From what happened next in the story, it sounds as though they are rather like a bat and a ball.

Gilgamesh called his friends: Enkidu and all the lads of Uruk had to come to the city square to play a game with the Elag and the Ekidmar, made from the roots of the same tree that had provided the shining throne and bed of the Goddess Inanna. All the mothers and sisters and aunts and cousins were required to come too, to watch the young men prove their skill and to provide the refreshments.

All day long, the young men played with the Elag and the Ekidmar – throwing and hitting, throwing and hitting;

endlessly entertaining for young King Gilgamesh. When the day was ending and the evening light was fading, very carefully Gilgamesh marked the spot where the ball last fell.

And the next day, not long after first light, he was up again with the lark and calling for his players and their supporters. But when the game started, in his enthusiasm Gilgamesh hit the Elag so hard that it flew right over the walls of Uruk and into the unknown regions beyond, down through the Gates of Ganza and into the Underworld itself: the region of the dead.

Gilgamesh was dismayed. 'My ball! I loved it! I was enjoying the game! I was nowhere near tired of it! Oh, if only it was yesterday! If only the wood was still in the woodwork shop! I would reward the woodworker, give gifts to his wife and daughter … now what will I do? Oh, great is my grief! Who will enter the gates of death and bring me back my ball?'

Then his friend Enkidu spoke. 'I'll go. I will fetch your ball from the region of death.'

'You'll go?'

'Yes.'

'You, Enkidu, would risk going into the Underworld, from which no one returns, and fetch back my ball?'

'Yes. I'll go.'

'Marvellous!' Gilgamesh was happy for his friend to go into the realm of death to get his ball back. 'But you realise that there are rules? If you keep the rules, you may go undetected, but if you break the rules, they will detect you and detain you. So, listen to the rules.'

'I'll listen.'

'Do not bathe and rub scented oils into your body.'

'I will not bathe and rub scented oils into my body.'

'Do not wear nice, new, clean clothes.'

'I'll not wear new clothes.'

'Do not wear nice new sandals.'

'I won't wear new sandals.'

'Under no circumstances make eye contact.'

'Won't make eye contact.'

'No hugging and kissing.'

'Won't hug or kiss.'

'And finally, don't drop anything and don't make a noise.'

'I won't drop anything or make a noise.'

'Keep to the rules and all may be well. But if you break them, they will detect you and detain you and we will never see each other again. I'll wait for you here.'

Enkidu rose up.

But, when Enkidu entered the Underworld, he broke all the rules, and he was recognised, detected and detained.

At the Gates of Ganza, Gilgamesh waited and waited, but his friend did not return, and then he knew that Enkidu had broken the rules and been detected and detained.

Weeping, he went to Enki in the Abzu, god of wisdom and fresh water. 'My friend Enkidu, whom I love, entered the Underworld and has been detained. I am Gilgamesh. Help my friend.'

Enki, kind and clever, spoke. 'Oh no! Your friend! We can't have that. What are rules, if not to be bent a little now and then? Each case is different and should be judged on its own merit.'

Enki called on Utu, the sun god. 'Utu! Shine a beam of uplifting sunlight! Make a hopeful opening! Send in a warm loving breeze.'

Utu, the sun god, shone a beam of sunlight and made an opening into the Underworld. He sent in a warm breeze. Gilgamesh watched as a sunbeam shone into the Underworld. Enkidu rose up, on the warm breeze and the sunbeam.

When Enkidu and Gilgamesh were reunited, there was hugging and kissing and a good few tears. The story says nothing more of the Elag and the Ekidmar. Gilgamesh saw then what was important and what was not.

As they walked, arm in arm, back to Uruk, Gilgamesh started wondering. He said, 'Enkidu, I find myself wondering. You are the only person who has ever gone into the land of the dead and returned. I'm wondering what it was like. Was it very terrible?'

'Very terrible indeed. There, I saw the one who was eaten by a lion: she searches perpetually for her hands and feet. The one who fell from the roof tries to match bone with bone. The one who dived and hit his head on the shipboard calls out, "Help me get this plank off my head!" The one who was burned in the fire is not there. His spirit has risen in smoke to the skies.'

'Did you see any of our old friends who have entered the Underworld?'

'Yes. I saw them.'

'Did you see the man who had seven sons?'

'Yes. I saw the man who had seven sons.'

'How does he fare?'

'How does he fare? He fares very well. He is like a king on a throne in the palace. He sits and hands out judgements.'

'Did you see the man who had six sons?'

'Yes. I saw the man who had six sons.'

'How does he fare?'

'He is as cheerful as the ploughman who drives his great ox through his own fields.'

'How about the man who had five sons?'

'Yes. I saw him.'

'How does he fare?'

'He is like the good scribe. He goes in and out of the palace as he pleases.'

'How about the rest?'

'The man who had four sons is as happy as the merchant who has four asses to carry his goods.

'The man who had three sons drinks fresh water from water skins.

'The man who had two sons doesn't fare so well. He sits on a couple of bricks to eat his bread.

'The man who had one son fares badly. He hammers a nail into the wall, and he weeps.'

'Did you see the man who had no sons?'

'Yes. I saw the man with no sons.'

'How does he fare?'

'He fares very badly. No food to eat. No water to drink. All he has is dust.'

'And Enkidu, what of the little children, my little ones, who never saw life at all?'

Enkidu said, 'I saw them. I saw your little ones. I saw the little children who never saw life.'

'How do they fare?'

'The little ones sit on seats of silver. They sit at tables of gold. They eat honey and butter, and they play all day. The Underworld echoes with the sound of their laughter.'

Then, hand in hand, Enkidu and Gilgamesh walked together. They were young men walking together, laughing like the little ones, hopeful, optimistic, walking towards their lives on the roads of endless sunlit days, away from the Gates of Ganza.

And always towards them.

10

GILGAMESH

By the water she sits. She is Siduri, the wise one, the healer, the herbalist. Her house is between the forest at the foot of the mountains of the sun and the ocean, which is the water of death.

She spends her days gathering herbs from the hillside. Then she lays them to dry in her sunny courtyard, or she chops them, or she pounds them with her pestle, and she makes them into healing medicines. She creates distillations, decoctions, infusions, extractions, tinctures, tisanes and refreshing teas, from what grows out of the earth. Then she puts them in pots and casks and urns and bottles, and stores them in the shade until someone comes who needs them.

One day Siduri, the wise woman, was resting in the courtyard. She raised her eyes to the garden of the gods, high on the hill, where the sun emerges from the mountains, and she saw a large creature clambering down the hillside towards her.

It was a man. He was enormous. His hair was wild. He was covered in dirt and dust. He was dressed in filthy, uncured lion skins. He was coming at a great speed towards her open doorway.

Quickly, she rose and pulled the big doors shut with a thud. She locked them and she bolted them and climbed the staircase to the roof terrace. The creature arrived at the big

She shut the doors.

gates below and, howling, hammered with both powerful fists. The whole house shook.

From the roof terrace, she called down, 'Who are you?'

He looked up at her. 'Who am I? I am Gilgamesh, the King of Uruk!'

She frowned and shook her head. 'If you are Gilgamesh, the King of Uruk, where is your crown, your robe, your retinue? If you are Gilgamesh, the King of Uruk, why are your eyes and your cheeks so hollow? Why are your lips cracked? Why is your skin grimy and your hair and beard matted with dirt? Why are you wearing uncured lion skins?'

He replied, 'My friend Enkidu, whom I loved: the doom of mortals came upon him, and he died. Now I am afraid of my own death. I seek my ancestor, Utnapishtim. He alone of all humankind knows the secret of immortality.'

It was no longer the matted hair, the dirt, that she saw. She saw suffering. She felt sorry for him.

Siduri, the wise woman, climbed down the steps to the courtyard. She walked past the drying herbs and the rows of pots and urns and bottles. She unbolted and unlocked the great doors and pulled them open.

She took the wild man by the arm and led him to a seat in the shade. She brought him a bowl of water and a cloth to wipe his face and she gave him a cup of cool spring water, with a few drops of something healing from a nearby cask. She sat down at his side and said, 'Tell me all about it.'

He bowed his head. 'I was the King of Uruk and the most powerful of all men. I had no equal. I was alone without a friend. One night I dreamed. In my dream, a meteor shot across the sky and fell at my feet. I saw it was an axe. I asked my mother the meaning of my dream.

'She said, "It's a good dream. The gods are sending you a true friend at last."

'And she was right. The gods sent me Enkidu the wild man. At first, we fought. But he was my equal. We became best friends. We were inseparable. We did everything together. We had adventures together, so many adventures.

'Together, we destroyed Humbaba, the Forest Guardian of the gods.

'Together, we killed the Bull of Heaven, sent to Earth by Inanna, Queen of Heaven and Earth.

'So many adventures. Too many adventures!

'Together we stained the white gown of the goddess with the blood of the bull. The gods were offended. They said someone should be punished. Someone should die.

'We killed the guardian and the bull together. But it was my friend alone who received the punishment. My friend Enkidu, whom I loved: the doom of mortals came upon him, and he died. He was punished. I was not.'

Siduri said, 'He does not suffer. It is you who suffers.'

Gilgamesh paid no heed to her words. 'For six days and

seven nights, I would not leave his side. I would not give him up for burial, until a worm crawled out of his nose. Then I gave his body to the priestesses. I called the craftsmen to make a statue of him: a statue of gold, carnelian, lapis and jade.

'After that, I lost all delight in city life. Then I became afraid that I too would die. I took to roaming alone in the wilderness, outside the walls of brick-built Uruk.

'One night, roaming under the full moon, I saw lions in the valley below. I was struck by terror and fury at one and the same time. I called on the moon god, 'Oh great god Nanna Suen! I will not lie down and die!'

She saw suffering.

'Then I fell on the lions. I killed them all. I took their skins and clothed myself. Then I spoke an oath in the light of the moon god. And these are the words I said: "I have an ancestor. His name is Utnapishtim. He alone of all mankind was granted immortality by the gods. I will find him. I will learn from him the secret of immortality. I will not die."

'Since then, I have searched. I have wandered in the wild land.

'I have stood at the gates of the Mountains of the Sun.

'I told my tale to the Scorpion People who guard the entrance. They were sorry for me, and they let me in.

'I have followed the path of the sun through the mountains. It took me twelve double hours, and the sun did not overtake me, till I stepped out, into the Garden of the Gods.

'I have walked in the Garden of the Gods, where the apples are rubies, and the grapes are amethyst. From the Garden of the Gods, I have seen your house by the sea. You sit here by the water. You are the wise healer! Heal me. Cure my pain. Relieve me of my suffering. Tell me where I will find my ancestor Utnapishtim. Tell me where he is. Tell me the way.'

Siduri heard the words of Gilgamesh. She was sorry for him. She said, 'Oh, Gilgamesh, why are you ceaselessly roaming? Why do you seek the life you never will find? Don't you know that when the great gods created humankind at the very beginning, immortality was a gift they kept for themselves? The gift they granted to humankind was death. Mortality.

'But with that ending, they gave other gifts: they gave the taste of this water, the sight of the sun sparkling on these waves, the cry of those seabirds.

'Gilgamesh, you are human and alive; use the great gifts of this earth for the benefit of all. Irrigate the land; grow dates; build homes; paint pictures; organise huge, wonderful projects for no reason at all – for delight.

'Gilgamesh, you are human and alive: dance and sing with your friends; enjoy a refreshing bath; comb scented oil into your hair; put on good clean clothes; enjoy good food; delight your beloved with your repeated embrace; hold the soft hand of your little child in yours.

'Because these things are also the gifts of the gods, and you are missing them all, in your useless search for the one thing you never can have.'

Gilgamesh looked at Siduri. He narrowed his eyes. He said, 'What are you talking about? Can you tell me where to find my ancestor, Utnapishtim, or can't you?'

For a moment the only sound was the waves washing on the shore. Then, from far off in the trees by the sea, there was the sound of axe on wood.

Siduri sighed and shook her head. She said, 'Listen. What can you hear?'

'I hear the sound of axe on wood.'

'Follow the sound. It is the sound of the ferryman fixing his boat. Follow the sound and find him. He alone knows the way. He can carry you over the dark waters to the land of your ancestor, Utnapishtim.'

'Well, why didn't you say so before? I'll go to my ancestor, Utnapishtim! He will teach me the secret of eternal life. Goodbye.' And he was up and out of the gates.

Siduri climbed the stairs and watched him as he raced along the salt seashore and disappeared into the trees. 'Oh, foolish human, why are you rushing and ceaselessly searching for the life you never can have? Build palaces, paint pictures, grow food, and dance, sing, laugh. Take your little child's hand in yours. Delight your beloved with your repeated embrace. Be happy. Be sad. But don't miss your life.'

But he was already rushing along the shore. He found the ferryman. He inadvertently destroyed the means of propulsion and was compelled to drive the ferry himself, first by pushing punting poles and then creating a sail with his lion-skin shirt and himself as the mast.

So, he reached the land of Utnapishtim, his ancestor.

Mr and Mrs Utnapishtim saw him from a long way off. Utnapishtim said, 'If you are Gilgamesh, the King of Uruk, where is your crown, your robe, your retinue? If you are Gilgamesh, the King of Uruk, why are your eyes and your cheeks so hollow; why are your lips cracked; why is your skin grimy and your hair and beard matted with dirt? Why are you wearing uncured lion skins?'

He replied, 'My friend Enkidu, whom I loved: the doom of mortals came upon him, and he died. Now I am afraid of my own death. I have come a long way seeking you. You, of all mankind, will live forever. Tell me the secret.'

They sat together. Utnapishtim said, 'I could summarise the story, but then the deeper truth would be lost. Stories are always embedded in other stories. In order for you to truly understand, I have to start at the beginning.

'In the beginning, the gods found the work of the earth very hard going. They weren't equipped to deal with her. So, they created humankind from her being. That's why we humans are so comfortable here. We're made of earth.

'But they added to the earth their own blood and spit, and that's why we're so uncomfortable here. We have the blood and the spit and the breath of the gods in us.

'In our comfort and discomfort, our species grew and populated the earth. And we were doing a great job, doing the work of the earth, but we were really noisy – the breath and spit and blood of the gods gave humankind a good strong voice, views and opinions.

'Enlil, the angry earth god, didn't like it.

'My guardian was Enki, the compassionate god of wisdom and fresh water. He heard the plan of Enlil, the angry earth god. The plan was to destroy humanity because of our noisiness. I was meditating and awake late at night and I heard a voice. It spoke to me from the walls of my reed-built house.

'It said, "Oh wall! I have a tale to tell. Enlil, the angry earth god, will destroy humanity. He will send plague, he will send drought, he will send flood. I have promised not to warn humanity. So, I am not. I am warning you, oh wall. Oh, if only Utnapishtim knew, he would build a big boat – a great big spherical coracle of a boat – and bring into it all the seeds and plants and insects and birds and beasts that are necessary to the maintenance of this marvellous world, and to humanity, whom we gods worked so hard to create."

'I was awake. I heard the words spoken to the reed wall. I carried out the instructions given to the reed wall. I survived the destruction. And so did my family, and all the plants and creatures I had saved.

'After forty days and forty nights of storm, I opened up the shutters of the boat and saw the grey water. There, all my good past companions were floating, all the good breath and the spit and the spirit – gone. Only the clay remained, floating on the surface, and sinking.

'When at last we reached land, I lit a fire and sent up blessings and gratitude. The sky lit up with the joy of the gods. They all gathered round. Even Enlil, the angry earth god, came. The rest of the gods faced the bully. They told him in no uncertain terms, "This must not happen again. If you're angry, send illness, send impotence. But not the wholesale destruction of our beloved humankind."

'And Enlil bowed to their decision and, in that moment, he granted me and the missus eternal life.

'Now you know. My dear direct descendant, Gilgamesh, I was awake, and I heard the words of my god and I followed his direction. Can you do the same? Can you be awake to hear the words of your god?'

Gilgamesh said, 'Yes! Of course! Here I am!' And instantly fell fast asleep.

Mrs Utnapishtim went to waken him. But Utnapishtim said, 'Let him sleep. He has travelled far. But while he sleeps, bake bread for him.'

When Gilgamesh awoke, he said, 'I'm not asleep. I was just resting my eyes.'

But Mrs Utnapishtim said, 'Oh Gilgamesh, while you slept, I baked. Each day, I baked.'

Beside the hearth, Gilgamesh saw six loaves of bread. The first was hot out of the oven. The second was cold. The third was hard, the fourth was dry. The fifth was spotted with white mould. The sixth was covered with green mould.

He saw the evidence of the passage of time in the decaying bread before him. And in it, saw too, the inevitability of his own mortality.

'Oh, Utnapishtim. What shall I do now? Where will I go now? Where will I lay my head? Wherever I look, death stands there. Wherever I go, there's death. Death lies here in the hearth. Death stands in my bedchamber and sits now by my side.'

Utnapishtim said, 'Yes. That's what it is to be human.'

He turned to the ferryman. He said, 'You no longer have a place here. Take Gilgamesh. Clean him up. Dress him properly. Take him home.'

Mrs Utnapishtim gave him a nudge, and Utnapishtim said, 'Alright. If you can find the sweet place in the poisoned water, there you will find the herb of youth. Swallow it and you will become, once more, the man you were in your youth.'

And Gilgamesh, warrior that he was, found the herb of youth in the deep waters. He found it, but he lost it again in the desert. He lost it to a little snake, who, before his eyes, swallowed it, sloughed off her skin and became once more the snake she had been in her youth.

At last, Gilgamesh accepted his ageing and his mortality and with it, his responsibility.

He entered into Uruk with his new friend, the ferryman. And began the proper work of a king.

Oh, foolish human.

Why are you rushing and ceaselessly searching for the life you never can have?

Build palaces, paint pictures, grow grain, eat food, dance, sing, laugh.

Take the little child's hand in yours.

Delight your beloved with your repeated embrace.

Be happy. Be sad. Don't miss your life.

9

Views of the Afterlife: The Medieval World of Chivalry

When we first set out to choose stories for this book, we felt that 'Orpheus and Eurydice', as an iconic story of love thwarted by death, was indispensable. Yet, in the end, we haven't included it. Instead of exploring the mythology of Ancient Greece, we have delved into Arthurian mythology and courtly love. The first story in this pairing is a medieval retelling of the Orpheus myth, while the second heralded the flowering, during the same period, of the concept of courtly love.

'Sir Orfeo' is a thirteenth century reimagining, originally written in rhyming couplets, of the Greek myth of 'Orpheus and Eurydice'. It brings a sweetness and a fairytale lightness to that dark myth, save perhaps for the grim vision of the 'taken ones' that Sir Orfeo sees in the fairy world, which is otherwise 'as bright as sun in summer air'.

Unlike the Greek myth, the Underworld in 'Sir Orfeo' is not populated by the dead. Instead, it is a place filled with people who have been taken away on the point of death, recalling the dead who are suspended in the limbo of their trauma, in Enkidu's Underworld.

Chrétien de Troyes' poem, called here 'Lancelot and the Hangman's Cart', is a romance of courtly love, exploring the nature of Lancelot's love for Guinevere. Chrétien credited Marie de Champagne as the source of the idea for this piece, which sparked a great outpouring of Arthurian literature throughout Europe. Several versions of the doomed relationship between Lancelot and Guinevere exist. In some, Lancelot is a faithful adherent to the rule of chivalry, in others the romantic devotee of an idealised love, or a passionate lover who betrays others for love of his Queen.

In addition to these medieval versions, some twentieth-century writers, for example Marion Zimmer Bradley, present the Arthurian women as more like goddesses and spirits than queens. This reading can be intuited by squinting between the medieval lines to more ancient versions of the tales, which may represent the gods and goddesses of Western Europe. In the retelling of the story offered here, Lancelot is a devotee of his goddess, and the castle where the queen is imprisoned is the Underworld.

Both these stories explore, in their own mythic worlds, an interweaving of the beliefs of the Christian Church, the conventions of courtly love and elements of much older Celtic stories. They are examples of the romances once shared by skilled minstrels and troubadours.

11

Sir Orfeo

Let me tell you of Sir Orfeo, who ruled a joyful, peaceful and fruitful kingdom with compassion and justice.

> Sir Orfeo was a king of old
> In England lordship high did hold;
> Valour he had, and hardihood,
> A courteous king, whose gifts were good.

His court was glorious and his people lived in peace and without fear. Sir Orfeo was descended from the gods of Greece, and his queen, the Lady Heurodis, was as fair, as graceful and as good a queen as anyone could wish for.

Sir Orfeo had a great love of music, and harp players were always welcome in his court. He was himself a fine harper – his touch on the strings brought melody and joy to all who heard.

This fine king and fair queen lived in Tracience, which the minstrels of old tell us became known as Winchester. Their story begins in early May, that time of promise and beauty, when buds and blossoms open and the days lengthen and warm.

On a fine May morning, Lady Heurodis went walking in the gardens of her palace with two of her maidens in attendance. As the day grew warm, she felt drowsy, so in the orchard she lay down, to the song of birds and the hum of bees. In the shade of a young, grafted tree, she fell asleep. Her maidens sat still and silent, not wanting to disturb her peaceful rest.

Time passed for them in a sleepy tranquil state, until suddenly Lady Heurodis began to scream. She sat bolt upright, although it was hard for the startled servants to tell whether she was awake or still asleep, and began to tear at her hair and thrash wildly about, until the grass and flowers were a muddy trampled mess.

Sir Orfeo had a great love of music.

Her maidens tried to calm her, and then to restrain her, but when it was clear that their efforts made no impression on the lady's alarming state, they ran back towards the palace, calling out for help: 'The queen is greatly troubled and we cannot bring her to herself!'

Courtiers and servants streamed out to the orchard, and seeing Heurodis's torments, her ladies gathered round her, reaching out to stroke her, murmuring endearments, as if to a child. But it took almost all of them to carry her indoors, as she writhed and screamed, and even when she was laid on her bed they still had to hold her back, time and again, from throwing herself down to the floor and racing away.

As soon as Sir Orfeo heard this dreadful news, he came running to Heurodis' side, more troubled than he had ever been in his life. He knelt beside her, surrounded by a small company of his most trusted knights, and spoke gently to her. 'My love, what troubles you so? You have ever been calm and peaceful, yet now you are in turmoil. You have torn your skin, your face is pale – and you stare at me with those dear eyes as if I were a stranger. I beg you, beloved, weep no more, but tell me what ails you, and what I can do to comfort you.'

Gradually, his familiar voice and gentle touch soothed Heurodis sufficiently for her to grow calm enough to speak. But her words were anything but calming, for either of them!

'O, my beloved lord,' she falteringly began, 'In my sleep I dreamed such a dream … We have been true to each other in life and love, and never have been parted. But now I am to be torn from you, and I am sure that my heart will break.'

'No, no,' protested Orfeo. 'Whatever makes you say this? We will never be parted, for where you go, there shall I go too!'

Heurodis answered bleakly. 'You cannot. This is my fate and mine alone. In my sleep, I dreamed a dream: two knights in silver armour came to me as I lay beneath a tree, in our own orchard. They commanded me to go with them to their lord's castle. I refused, in no uncertain terms, at which they rode away to take my answer to their king.

'The next moment, the whole court of this lord arrived – scores of knights, and lovely ladies too, each finely clad. They were all dazzling and shining bright, and the brightest of them all was their king, who wore a crown of light, not made of silver or gold, but carved from a single glowing gem.

'He looked fair, but his deeds were anything but pleasing to me. He caught me up and set me on a horse at his side. He took my reins, all that host closed about me, and I was forced to ride with them to his palace.

'It was a wonderful place, surrounded by beautiful lands, but it pleased me not to be there against my will. He showed me everything without a word, then brought me back to our orchard. Only then did he speak, and his words filled me all anew with dread.

'"Lady," he said,

"Without fail, tomorrow you must be
Waiting here beside this tree.
Away with us you then shall ride,
And with us always you will bide.

No matter how you try to avoid this fate, be assured, we will take you, and if need be, we shall tear you limb from limb, and even so, in pieces, we will carry you away."'

Sir Orfeo listened in growing horror and swore that he would sooner lose his life than his beloved. He gathered all his advisors to counsel him, but none of them knew what to do. His only conclusion was that he must defend Heurodis with all the might at his command.

And so it was that, the next day, at the appointed time, Heurodis stood pale and trembling under the tree, inside a ring of knights who stood shoulder to shoulder, their circle bristling with drawn swords, and outside them a second

A crown of light.

circle, with spears at the ready. Sir Orfeo, grim-faced, was at his lady's side, with both her hands clasped closely in his.

But it was all to no avail.

Without a sign or a sound, suddenly she was no longer there! Heurodis vanished utterly, transported by a magic more powerful than any of them could understand.

Sir Orfeo was bereft. That very day, he called his steward to him and spoke words that further horrified the court. 'Into your hands I put the care of the kingdom,' he said. 'You have been faithful and true to me throughout my long years of kingship, so now I charge you to take my place, and rule this kingdom wisely and well. I can no longer stay here without my beloved Heurodis, for everything reminds me of all I have lost. I have determined to go out into the barren lands to grieve for her and live as a hermit. If word comes to you that I have died, then summon all the wise ones of the realm to a parliament and name my successor.'

The steward was as noble as his master and begged to be excused, urging his lord to stay. But the bleak look in Orfeo's eyes could not be denied. Finding that all his prayers and entreaties made no difference to his lord's determination, at last the good steward fell silent, and bowed his head in humble obedience to this great fate.

Then Sir Orfeo said farewell to all his courtiers, who wept bitter tears and begged him to stay. But he could not be gainsaid, and so went for the last time from that great hall. In his chamber, he stripped off all his finery, abandoned his weapons and, dressed only in a tattered cloak, he left the palace on bare feet. Only one thing of all his riches went with him: on his back he carried his beloved harp.

No one tried to stop him. The citizens of the city lined the streets, faces wet with tears and heads bowed low in acknowledgment of his, and their, terrible loss.

Orfeo left his kingdom without a backward glance, and set out into the barren moorlands, where he began a hard and bitter life.

Instead of soft furs and velvet clothes, he wore tatters and rags.

Instead of a fine feather bed, he slept curled up on bracken and moss.

Instead of dining on all manner of sweetmeats, he grubbed for roots and gathered berries.

Instead of being surrounded by a glittering throng of courtiers, he was alone, far from sight or sound of other humans.

For ten long years, Orfeo endured great hardship, and it

marked his body, though not his spirit. His tangled hair and beard grew long and wild, his nails crooked and curved like claws, his skin was darkened by the sun and toughened by the wind and weather. His clothing wore away to rags, until he had only animal pelts to shield his nakedness from the elements. He lived like some savage beast, in all ways but one.

Now and again, when some sweet or sad emotion overwhelmed him, he would tune his harp, settle his fingers on the strings and play. The sound would draw the birds and beasts to him, so that he played at the centre of a still circle of all manner of living things.

Those ten years passed without the sight of another human. Sometimes, it seemed to Orfeo as if a host of hunters passed by, with hounds in full cry and horns sounding; or a regiment, as if of knights, marched through with banners flying; or courtiers seemed to come a-dancing, to the beat of tabour and tambourine. But Orfeo knew they were fairy folk, from the court of the lord who had spirited away the Lady Heurodis. The wood wisdom that Orfeo gained from this long apprenticeship to nature stood him in good stead, and he ignored these sights as if they were but visions, wondering indeed whether, in truth, that was all they were.

Until one day, a fateful day, a group of ladies rode by, with falcons on their wrists, and a playful mood came over Orfeo, so that he cried aloud:

'By the rood, this is a merry throng,

And I with them will go along,

To see these brave birds fly and watch the sport,

For skilful feats will sure be wrought.'

So Orfeo followed the riders down to the water meadows where, coming closer to them, he recognised his dear Heurodis!

At first, he thought that what he saw must be a waking dream or a vision of his love-starved heart, but it was clear that she was really there, for her gaze locked with his, she moved her lips – though no words came – and her eyes brimmed with tears, as she took in the hardship written on his face and form and saw how he had suffered by her loss.

She went to move towards him, but the women with her prevented this, and with one accord they closed their horses tight around hers, recalled their falcons to the jesses and forcibly turned her horse, pressing against its flanks and withers and then cantering away, with her trapped in the middle of the throng.

Orfeo now lamented his fate most bitterly and swore he deserved to die, having seen his long-lost wife without speaking a single word to her. But then he declared:

'For life and death no more I care,
And I will follow where they fare.
To search for her I now will dare,
Heurodis' fate at last to share.'

Snatching up his precious harp, he went after them as fast as he could and saw them pass through a door in the side of a great, green hill. He followed them fearlessly, penetrating deep into that rock, until he came at last into another land.

It was as bright there as sun in summer air and a great verdant plain opened before him. He saw on that plain a castle, surrounded by a crystal wall, with towers standing proud all about it, each supported by a golden buttress. Every inch of that palace, it seemed, was richly adorned with carvings and the inner chambers were walled with gems. Night never fell there, for every stone shone with the light of dawn.

It seemed to Orfeo as fine as any place that might be in heaven. Yet heaven it assuredly was not, as he soon discovered, for he went straight to the gate and knocked. A porter came and courteously asked his business.

Orfeo replied equally courteously, saying, 'I am a minstrel, come to offer my music to the lord of this place, if he pleases to listen.'

The porter opened wide the gate, and Orfeo went in.

Then he saw.

He saw all the gloom and glamour and terror of that place. He saw the taken ones who had been drawn there, as Heurodis had been. They were not dead, yet they were mourned as lost in the world above.

He saw people with limbs missing or terrible wounds; some who had burned and some who had drowned; some who had been strangled and others who were raving in the chains that bound them, while others again lay peacefully, as if in sleep. There were warriors in armour and women in labour, each one where and how he or she had been when that fairy lord's magic had caught them and brought them to this land. And then he saw her: his own dear Heurodis, asleep beneath the apple tree in their orchard.

When he reached the great hall, where the lord and lady of that dread place sat in state, with crowns of shining gems upon their brows, Orfeo knelt humbly before the king and said, 'My Lord, I am a minstrel, and if you permit, I will play for you.'

The king was astonished. 'What are you doing here?' he asked. 'I have not summoned you. Never, since I came to power, has any human dared to come here without my summons. Yet, you are here, of your own free will. What has brought you, in defiance of all sense?'

'Lord,' replied Orfeo, 'I assure you that I am nothing more, or less, than a poor wandering minstrel. It is our custom to come unbidden to the halls of great lords, and even when we find small welcome, we nonetheless offer our gift of music.'

With that, Orfeo sat down and tuned his harp. And then he began to play.

Every being in the hall, whether living, dead or taken, was drawn to the sound. They gathered around him, entranced by the beauty of his music. The king sat silent, enrapt and delighted, and both he and his queen found great joy in Orfeo's music.

When the last notes had faded, the king stirred himself and spoke:

'Minstrel, your music pleases me.

'I'll grant your wishes as your fee.

'Freely your request I'll pay.

'Come ask, and I'll prove what I say.'

This was Orfeo's chance, and this the end towards which he had aimed. He drew a deep breath, and spoke:

'Lord, I beg you, give to me

'The lady, beautiful to see,

'Who sleeps beneath the apple tree.'

The king gave a scornful laugh. 'That would never do,' he jeered, 'for she is faultless, fine and fair, while you are rough and ragged. It would be a monstrous thing to see her in your company.'

Orfeo responded courteously but boldly. 'Lord, it would be far more monstrous to see a noble king, such as you, renege on your word. You cannot deny – with all these witnesses about us – that you offered me free choice for my reward. For your honour, you should keep your word.'

This king lived by his own code, and though it seems a strange one to us humans, yet he held his word to be sacred. 'Very well, then, let it never be said that I do not honour my word. Take her hand and go. And I wish you both joy, my friend.'

Orfeo thanked the lord most fervently, and then, hand in hand with Heurodis, he left that strange kingdom and brought her back to our human world.

Their road was long, but at last they came once more to their own city of Tracience. However, they sent no word of their return ahead to court. Indeed, when they reached the outskirts of the city, Orfeo found and rented a mean little room – the sort of lodging a wandering minstrel might manage to afford.

While Heurodis rested there, Orfeo asked around among the poor folk of that place for news of the kingdom, as if he were a stranger there. He heard his own story from the mouths of his people, how their queen had been stolen away and their king had abandoned his throne, because he could not bear to stay without her. He heard how a steward now ruled the land, and that he was a fair and just lord.

Orfeo was glad of all he heard. After he had found out as much as he could, he set out for the palace, his harp across his back, leaving Heurodis still hidden in their lodgings. High men and low turned away from him as they passed him in the street, exclaiming in disgust at his filthy rags, his tangled hair and beard, his dirty feet and hands. Orfeo said not a word to anyone, kept his gaze low and his steps straight ahead, until he chanced to see the steward of the land. Then he called out: 'My lord, I am a harper from far away. Please have mercy on me in my distress.'

The steward turned a kindly gaze towards him.

'My lord and master loved to play the harp,' he said in a gentle voice. 'For his sake, I would never see a harper suffer. Come with me.' The steward led Orfeo to the great hall of the court and he was given a place at the table among the servants, to eat his fill and gather his strength.

The steward took his place at the high table and, after the feast, he signalled to the court musicians. Trumpet and tabour, fiddle and harp played, and Orfeo listened from his seat low down in the hall and said not a word. But when the court musicians had withdrawn, he tuned his harp, put his fingers to the strings and began to play. All eyes turned towards him and every voice was silenced as they were caught up in his music.

The steward stared and stared, and he knew the harp. He called out:

'Minstrel, I bid thee, tell me true,

'How came this noble harp to you?

'For it recalls one I once knew.'

Then Orfeo spun a tale almost as strange as his own true story, telling the lord of how he had wandered the world for ten years, and how, all that time ago, he had come to a shallow valley. There, on the desert floor, he had found the body of a man who had been torn apart by wolves or lions. A harp lay beside the corpse.

'And this,' he concluded, 'is the harp I found that day.'

The steward cried out as if in pain. 'O woe is me! That was Sir Orfeo, my own true master. How shall I bear it, to know that he suffered such a cruel fate?' The steward fell to the ground in despair. His courtiers helped him rise, murmuring that death comes to us all, in many forms, and cannot be avoided.

Now Orfeo knew that his steward was loyal and true, that he had governed well and his heart was still full of love and loyalty to his lord. He stood up, and in ringing tones he spoke out: 'Steward, if your king, Orfeo, were here, if he had found and rescued his queen from the enchantment of fairy land, if he had come to your court in disguise to know whether you ruled well and true, he would have come ready to weigh up all that he found. If I were him, I would be well pleased by all that I had seen and heard today. And indeed, I am him: your own king come home at last, and I swear that for your fidelity, I shall name you my successor.'

Then at last everyone knew their king, in spite of his changed appearance, and the loyal steward threw himself at his lord's feet. A cry went up, as if with one voice: 'Sir Orfeo, our lord and king!'

Then servants took Orfeo to his chamber and bathed and shaved and robed him. When he was ready, a procession set out to bring home Heurodis, who was waiting for news of how the people had received him.

They brought her into town with merry songs and minstrelsy, and Sir Orfeo and Lady Heurodis were crowned anew.

They lived long and joyfully, King and Queen of Tracience once more, and when at last they died, the steward ruled after them.

The harpers of Britain told this story
Of Orfeo in all his glory.
A lay they made of fair delight,
And after the king they named it right.
And now Sir Orfeo's tale is done
So fine it shines, beneath the sun.

Reunited.

12

LANCELOT AND THE HANGMAN'S CART

Guinevere was sovereign queen of the land, and queen to good King Arthur.

One fair May morning, Queen Guinevere and all her ladies decided to have a pleasant picnic in a forest clearing and watch the summer coming in. They sat among the hawthorn trees and admired the gay May blossom there.

Then from the darkest part of the wood, where winter still reigned, came the cruel Lord Maleagant. The Queen of Life was surrounded, taken below and imprisoned beyond the gates in the dark realm of the otherworld.

All the land was laid waste. The people mourned and bewailed the loss of the queen. All save Lancelot and Gawain. They did not waste time be-wailing, but instead went riding out on a quest, though they had no idea which way to go.

Along the way they met with a hangman's cart.

'Hello, lords!' said the little man who drove the cart. 'I know just who you're looking for and just where she is, and I'll tell you this for nothing. The only way you will enter into that realm is riding in this cart.'

Now, to travel in the cart of ignoble death is of great shame to anyone, let alone a knight of Arthur's table. Gawain would not countenance it. And even Lancelot hesitated. A noble death held no fears for him, but an ignoble one was worse than death. Yet his hesitation was momentary. He climbed into the cart. Stripped of all honour and respect, tormented by the jeers and cat calls of the crowd, he rode the hangman's cart along the road, through the gates of death and into the realms below.

In the shadows there, he found his queen. Joyfully he rushed towards her, but she withdrew from him.

'Oh Lancelot. You hesitated. You chose honour rather than my light and love.'

But then she relented. She stepped towards him. 'Yet your hesitation was momentary and so shall be my restraint.' She embraced him. He was permitted to lead her back into this world.

In the world, the light returned, the land was restored and there was much celebration at this restoration. And so it is that we too can sit among the hawthorn trees and admire the gay May blossom and celebrate the summer coming in.

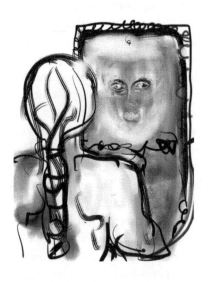

In the shadows, he found the queen.

THE DARK HUMOUR
OF DEATH

Sometimes humour gives us a chance to approach a diffi-cult subject by making it less daunting. Here are two comic stories about death. One is full of dark humour, while the other is more slapstick in its style.

The story 'Sam'l and the Great Worm' is one of ten Lincolnshire stories collected by Marie Balfour in the 1880s, which she published in the Folklore Society's journal *Folklore* in 1891. These stories are, as a group, very unlike other British folk tales, and some folklorists believed that Balfour created them herself. However, Maureen James, in her PhD research into the stories, refuted this idea, using census records and detailed study of local dialect words to tentatively identify some of the contributors. Some stories came from conversations that Balfour initiated with patients in her doctor husband's waiting room. She heard the story included here from a 9-year-old girl named Fanny.

James suggests that the dark imagery of many of the tales – and 'Sam'l' is a good example of this macabre story world – may have been due to the widespread use of opium as a remedy for malaria in the marshy Carrs of Lincolnshire.

Whatever its source, the dark and oppressive afterlife presented in this story makes one shudder.

Is the concept of the afterlife as a terrible and gloomy state part of humankind's collective unconscious? And if so, how do humans manage to hold this view in tandem with the vision of eternal joy and reward held out by many world religions? Could humour be part of the answer?

The story we have put in partnership with 'Sam'l' makes light of the subject of death through the actions of its foolish central character, who believes he is dead simply because he is told that he is.

The Mullah Nasreddin, also known as the Hodja, is a well-known figure in the folklore of the Islamic world. Indeed, you can attend a week-long festival held in his honour every year in July in Aksehir, in Turkey. This is where he died, in or about 1285.

A Mullah is a holy man in Islam, and should be a wise person. Indeed, Hodja is an honorific title bestowed on a teacher. But Nasreddin is a wise fool, and his stories teach through humour. Often, it is Nasreddin himself who is the butt of the joke.

As George Borrow wrote in 1884, in his book about Nasreddin, *The Turkish Jester*, 'Some people say that, whilst uttering what seemed madness, he was, in reality, divinely inspired, and that it was not madness but wisdom that he uttered.'

In this spirit, we include an example of the Mullah's teaching stories as an antidote to the gloomy vision of the first tale.

13

Sam'l and the Great Worm

It was a bad day when Sam'l died, for he was caught in a house fire and burnt to death, and everyone says that's a terrible way to go. I wouldn't know, but I expect they are right. To be honest, though, things didn't get really bad for Sam'l until after that.

It took him a while to work out what had happened and where he was – and indeed, what he was, since his body was nowhere to be seen, and everything seemed so strange, for there were bogles and all kinds of things like that about him. But he got up – well, what had been inside him got up, if you see what I mean, and he gave himself a shake, what there was of him to shake, and he wondered what he ought to do next.

And by and by, one of the things that were about said to him, 'You must go in the earth place, and tell the Big Worm that you're dead, and ask him to have yourself eaten up, or you'll never get to rest in peace.'

'Oh, is that what it is?' said Sam'l. 'Well, I'm willing.'

Now, Sam'l had been an obedient sort of a fellow in life, so he set out, asking his way, to find this Big Worm, and he'd have had to rub shoulders (if he'd still had any) with all the horrid things that glowered around him. After a while, he came to a great, dark place with glimmering lights crossing it. It was full of an earthy smell – and whiffs of a much worse stink, too. Under his feet (if he'd had any) there were creeping things, and all around there were crawling fluttering things, and the air felt hot and mucky.

At the far end of that place was a horrid great worm, coiled up on a flat stone, with its slimy head swinging from side to side as though it were sniffing out its dinner.

Suddenly, Sam'l's name was called aloud into that great silence, and he felt pretty scared when the worm shot out its horrible head, right into where his face would have been, if he'd had one. 'So, it's you, Sam'l. So, you're dead and buried, and food for us worms? Where's your body, then?' enquired the Worm.

Well, needless to say, Sam'l didn't want to get on the wrong side of this worm, so he answered politely. 'Please, Your Worship, here I am.'

'No,' said the Worm. 'Do you think we can eat what there is of you here? You're dead, lad, and you must fetch us your body for us to eat it up, if you want to rest in peace.'

'Please, your worship, here I am.'

'But where is it? My body, I mean,' said Sam'l, and he would have scratched his head, if he'd still had one.

'Well, where is it buried?' asked the Worm.

'It isn't buried, that's just it,' said Sam'l. 'It's ashes. It was all burnt up in the fire.'

'Oh, that's bad,' said the Worm. 'You won't taste so good. But don't fret, go and fetch the ashes, and bring them here. Us'll do the best we can.'

It did sound like a daunting task to Sam'l, but he promised he would also do the best he could. He set off to find the place where the house had been. When he got there, he sorted and sifted through all the ash of all the walls, and the roof beams, and the furniture, and the other people (that wasn't very nice), until he reckoned he'd gathered up all the ashes that were all of him – and none of anyone else, because that would be a right awkward mistake to make. He scraped his whole self into a sack and carried it back to the Great Worm.

The Great Worm pushed its head into the mouth of the sack, slithered around and sniffed and snuffed, turning over the ashes. Sam'l could see it wasn't too happy.

'You're not all here, Sam'l,' complained the Worm.

'Well, Your Highness, I reckon I collected up everything that was there. I know it's a bit mixed up, like, but I've got everything I could find.'

But the Great Worm would not have its expert opinion doubted. 'No, Sam'l, there's something missing. Where's the rest of you? You'll have to seek it. There's a whole armful not accounted for.'

'Ah, well, yes, that's right,' said Sam'l respectfully. 'It wouldn't be here, because it wasn't in the fire. It was cut off by the sawbones, it was, a good long time ago.'

'You'll have to find it, Sam'l, we must have the whole of you here.'

Sam'l tried to scratch his head, but he couldn't, because he didn't have one. 'Sir, I'll do my best, but I don't know where the doctor put it once it was off. Still,' he offered, 'I'll go and look.'

So, he looked here and he looked there, until, by-and-by, he did come across it.

Back came Sam'l and presented his arm to the Worm.

The Worm turned it over. And over.

'It's still not all here, Sam'l. Think now. Have you ever lost anything else?'

Sam'l thought hard. 'I did lose a nail,' he said. 'When I was a lad I hit my thumb with a hammer, and the nail came right off and never grew again.'

'That's it, then, I reckon,' said the Worm. 'You need to find that nail for me, Sam'l.'

Sam'l puffed out his non-existent cheeks. 'I can't see as I'll ever find that,' he said, 'but I'm willing to try.' And off he went.

But a nail is an easy thing to lose and a hard thing to find, and he could not track it down, try as he might.

At last, he had to go back to the Worm. 'I've sought it here and there and everywhere,' he reported dolefully, 'and I've not found it. But a nail is not much of a thing. Could you not take me without it? It's no great loss, is it? Can't you maybe manage without it, as I did all those years?'

'No, Sam'l, that I cannot,' replied the Great Worm decisively. 'I just can't. And if you can't find it – are you *sure* you've looked everywhere?'

'Sure and certain, worse luck, Sir!'

'You'll have to walk the Earth then, till you do find it.'

'But what if I can't find it?' Sam'l was beginning to panic.

'Then you'll have to walk for all time. I'm very sorry for you, Sam'l, but at least you'll have plenty of company.'

All the creeping things and the crawling things gathered companionably about Sam'l at those words, and ever since, unless he's found his nail – which I doubt – he's still walking the Earth searching for it.

And maybe there's a message here for all the rest of us. But if there is, I can't think what it might be.

14

THE HODJA AND HIS DEATH

In his later days, the Hodja became preoccupied by a big question. 'When am I to die?'

Repeatedly, he asked himself the question. He got no answer.

Repeatedly, he asked God. He got no answer.

Repeatedly, he asked his wife.

She said, 'There's life and energy in you in the here and now, and while you've got it, put it to good use. Look to the scriptures. Calm your heart. Look within. Do what's necessary. Do your duties about the house.'

But still he asked, 'When? When?'

At last, his wife had had enough of it. She said, 'Enough. I've been on at you about that overhanging branch on the old sycamore at the end of the yard for months. Get out there and cut it off before it has someone's eye out.'

Grumbling, the Hodja began the task. He propped the ladder up against the trunk, strapped the saw to his back and climbed up and out, onto the branch. He shuffled along on his bottom and began to saw away at the place where the branch joined the trunk, muttering to himself in time with the rhythm of the saw, 'When am I to die? When am I to die?'

A traveller passed along the path below. He called a greeting up to the Hodja. 'Take care friend. If you carry on like that, there's a nasty tumble ahead of you.'

'Mind your own business and go on your way!' barked the Hodja.

The traveller shrugged and walked up the path and out of sight, while the Hodja resumed his sawing and muttering. Almost immediately, the branch, weakened by the sawing, creaked under the weight of the Hodja. Suddenly there was a crack.

The branch broke, and both the branch and the Hodja tumbled onto the path. He clambered out from the foliage and sat rubbing his bruises. Then, with dawning amazement and delight, he stood up and began to limp and wobble up the road, calling, 'Stranger! Traveller! Friend!'

Ahead, the traveller stopped and turned, and the Hodja caught up.

'What a seer you are!' cried the Hodja.

'What do you mean?'

'You foretold the future!'

'Foretold the future?'

'You told me I would tumble – and tumble I did!'

The traveller raised an eyebrow.

'Oh, great seer, who predicts the future, now I have a great question for you. Please answer the question that has been preoccupying me these many days.'

The traveller frowned, perplexed.

'No! Tell me! You can do it! Answer me this: When am I to die?'

The traveller looked incredulous, shook his head and, turning away, took a few steps down the path, but the Hodja was hobbling in front of him.

'Don't go!' he said. 'Tell me. Tell me.'

'How should I know?'

'I will not let you pass till you tell me. When am I to die? When am I to die? I must have an answer!'

At last, exasperated by the Hodja's tenacity, the traveller

blurted out, 'If you must have an answer, I will give you an answer. Let the answer be: you will die after your donkey has farted three times!'

Satisfied, the Hodja allowed the traveller to pass and watched him walk away. Then, with horror, he shrieked, 'But I fed the donkey beans for breakfast!'

As quickly as he could, he scrambled back to the stable, where the donkey dozed contentedly. As soon as the donkey saw him, it brayed and farted loudly.

'Agh! Once!' cried the Hodja, and he ran behind the donkey and tried to clamp its tail down over its rear. But the donkey brayed and kicked and farted again.

'Agh! Twice!' cried the Hodja. Frantically, he began improvising ways to stop his donkey farting.

He gathered handfuls of hay.

He called, 'Wife! Bring bottle stoppers from the kitchen!'

She called, 'What? Why?'

He screeched, 'Bottle stoppers now!'

He improvised a complicated nappy system from ropes, but when he tried to apply it to the donkey's bottom, the donkey brayed and kicked and promptly farted a third time.

'Agh! Three!'

The Hodja's wife entered the stable with a bottle stopper in her hand, just in time to see the Hodja fall to the floor with an anguished cry. He lay still.

She hurried to his side and shook him. 'Husband! What's wrong? Are you alright?'

The Hodja opened one eye to her and said, 'Of course I'm not alright. Can't you see I'm dead?'

'Really? You don't sound dead.'

'Take my word for it. My donkey has farted three times. It has been foretold. I am dead and it is now your duty to arrange the funeral.'

'But …'

'That's the end of it. Donkey. Funeral.' And he closed his eye, lay still and did not speak.

Later, she returned to check on him. He lay perfectly still.

'Husband …'

'Funeral!'

She shrugged, went into the house to get a handkerchief and set off to visit the neighbours, weeping loudly as she entered their yard. 'Oh, my poor husband! The Hodja is dead. I must arrange his funeral.'

All the neighbours gathered round to comfort her and they worked together to help with the necessary ceremony. And all were soon in a sad procession to the burial ground.

Everything was going wonderfully well, until they came to the fork in the road. Here, a disagreement arose. There were two routes: one was a long and beautiful road with plenty of time for companionship and contemplation. The other was a short and dusty road.

The men wanted to go down the short road so they could get to the coffee shop afterwards and gossip in comfort. But the women wanted to go by the long, pretty road and enjoy the view.

The pall bearers were getting quite animated by the discussion and put down their burden to join in properly. But as they did, there was a cry from the corpse.

The Hodja sat up, pulled the shroud off his face and announced, 'It's my funeral. If I was alive, I'd agree with the men. Let's go the short way!'

At which his wife replied, 'Well you're not alive. You're dead. Behave. Lie down!' And she hit him hard on the head with a handy stick. The Hodja fell dead for the second time that day.

So they all went the pretty way.

'It's my funeral.'

CAN LOVE BE STRONGER THAN DEATH?

Here are the two stories to which we have been drawn – from very many possibilities – to explore that most human and optimistic question: Can love be stronger than death?

The cynical answer, of course, is 'only in stories', where the phrase 'ever after' is linked to 'happiness'. We can't live happily ever after, but perhaps we can live happily in the present moment. These two stories speak to our need to make the lost loved one present in some way, so that we can continue to both care for them and be cared for by them.

In 'The Long Welsh Tramping Road', the saints and the saviour of Christian mythology are characterised as folk-tale figures. Fiona writes:

I first heard this story told in Welsh by bilingual story-teller Tamar Eluned Williams, and was intrigued by its take on Christian beliefs. Trying to learn more about it, and keen to include it in this book, I eventually tracked down a version in a collection of Welsh folk tales on my own bookshelf. It seems that only when the story became relevant for me, did I find it. Its irreverent approach to the belief system in which I grew up was very appealing. But more than that, after losing my own partner and arranging his funeral, Elen's determination to do right by Jonah, even beyond death, was something that I could at last understand.

June writes:

The second story, 'Savitri and Satyavan', comes from the great Sanskrit epic *The Mahabharata*, with which I have worked over many years, alone and with others. The story I have chosen here is a frame tale within one of its many episodes, which between them explore a whole range of human experience and emotions.

In the Vedas, poetry from 1500 BCE, death is characterised as Lord Yama, the first human to tread the path of mortality. Since that time, all human beings have followed in his footsteps, but only he has the right to sit in judgement. He is the cheerful king of the departed ancestors. Later representations depict him as a judge of behaviour in the life that has been lived.

In this story, Lord Yama is implacable, all-powerful, yet not immune to flattery, and scrupulously fair, as you will see, even when caught out by Savitri's clever wish.

15

The Long Welsh Tramping Road

The Long Welsh Tramping Road stretches all the way from the blazing fires and dirty smoking chimneys of 'Fernal to the tall roofs and sunny streets of High Eden.

About midway between the two there was, for a long time, a cottage with the door all painted black with tar to keep out the weather, where there lived a pair of pensioners named Elen and Jonah. Elen was a tidy old soul, and got on well enough with all the neighbours, even nosy old Mrs Ogmore, but no one had a good word to say about Jonah. Apart from Elen, who always tried to see the best in everyone.

But Jonah didn't care one way or the other what anybody thought of him, or whether or not he treated people well, until the night came when he had a dream. In that dream, he stood among the smoke-grimed chimneys of 'Fernal, and a great red voice called out, 'Welcome home, Jonah!'

Dream Jonah looked around and, having a bad feeling about the place, he asked in a thin and quavering voice, 'But where is home?'

And the voice replied cheerfully, 'Home to Blazes, Jonah. Where else, but home to Blazes?'

Dream Jonah trembled so much that he woke himself up, but even when the dream was gone, the voice still echoed in his mind like an ominous portent. He turned to Elen and said to her, 'O Elen, I am not long for this world, that is for sure. And I am terrible afraid of the 'Fernal fires down there below. Promise me, promise me, that when I'm gone you will see my soul safe into the High Place above.'

'Jonah,' said Elen stoutly, 'For sure, you aren't the snowiest flake that ever fell from Heaven, but you aren't the worst villain that ever lived, either. Not by a long chalk. I'll do my very best for you.'

It was only a day or two later that Jonah took sick. Truth to tell, the dream had knocked the stuffing out of him, and it wasn't long before they both knew in their hearts that he was definitely on the way out.

For the next week, Elen sat by his bedside, day and night. She held a leather bag close to his face. When he finally gave up the ghost, it drifted out of his mouth and slid into the bag with a tired sigh. Immediately, Elen snapped into action, tying the neck of the bag tightly. Then she slung it over her shoulder with a determined look on her face.

The bag was heavy, heavier than she had expected, for Jonah had been a short sort of man, but Elen was undaunted. She fed and petted their corgi and set him to guard the place, leaving the door of the barn open so he could get in for

She set the corgi to guard the door.

shelter. Then she went out, closing her front door carefully behind her. She put the key under the stone, as usual, and set off along the Long Welsh Tramping Road, her back to smoky 'Fernal and her face towards High Eden.

She had only been going for an hour and a minute when she came to a place where a bridge was down. There seemed no way to carry on. Leaning on the ruined parapet was a singularly odd-looking fellow, his face smudged with coal dust, the tiny tips of two horns poking out of his careful comb-over and what was definitely a tail protruding from the hem of his overcoat.

'In my dark name,' said the stranger, 'Give me Jonah's soul, which rightly belongs to me, or you shall go no further.'

The bag on Elen's back wriggled and writhed at that, but Elen was unperturbed. 'Surely, Lord Blazes,' she answered, 'You know that I was Jonah's better half, for a long time. Why do you want the worse half?'

While the stranger struggled to formulate an answer, Elen pressed home her advantage, using skills honed by years of haggling in the market. 'Now,' said she, 'Tell me, for I know you are a quick worker, what is the best price you can give me for throwing a new bridge over this pit?'

'Elen,' said he, 'I have too much at stake here to play for matchsticks, but if the first living thing to cross shall be mine for all eternity, then a bridge you shall have – and pronto!'

'Pronto it is,' said Elen, taking and shaking his hot hand to seal the bargain.

Once the bridge called Pronto spanned the pit, which really did take no time at all, Elen put her fingers in her mouth and blew a shrill whistle. It resounded all the way back down the Long Welsh Tramping Road to the little house with the tarred front door. Her corgi pricked up his ears at once, knowing that she had a job for him. He was bounding up the road to Elen's side before the dark stranger knew what she was about. She took up a stick and threw it across the bridge. Tail wagging eagerly, the corgi darted across and retrieved it, coming back as pleased as Punch, with the stick in its mouth.

The bridge builder glared at the little dog for a long moment, but then he shook his head in rueful admiration. 'Well, Elen,' he said, 'You were too clever for me that time, and no mistake. But let it never be said that Lord Blazes rats on a bargain.'

And with that, he reached down to take hold of the corgi by its scruff. But the corgi knew a bad'un when it saw one. It was ready for him. It snapped and nipped until his hot hand ran red with blood, and he pulled away, cursing between gritted teeth. 'To Heaven with your corgi!' he yelled and disappeared in a blaze of fire and a stink of brimstone.

Elen patted the corgi, gave him the scraps from the bottom of her pocket and sent him home. Then, chuckling and groaning all at once, she shouldered her burden once more and carried on, across the bridge, on her way.

When she arrived at High Eden, she stopped to catch her breath, and put down the leather bag to rest her shoulders. This, however, caused the bag to squirm and squiggle in some distress, so that she had to pick it up again.

She took a deep breath, went up to the front door and knocked. A man came bustling out in a businesslike way. She knew by the bunch of keys on his belt that this must be Saint Peter.

She greeted him politely. 'Good morning, Blessed Peter. I have brought you the soul of my husband Jonah. I expect you will have heard of him. I've come to ask you to take him into High Eden.'

Peter shook his head. 'No one by the name of Jonah ever proved to be much good, and yours is one of the fishiest of them all. The list of complaints against him is as long as my arm. I am sorry to tell you this, when you have come so far, but there is no place for such as Jonah here in High Eden.'

Elen looked at him then with different eyes and her voice took on a hint of steel, which the market traders back at home would have recognised at once. 'Jonah may have been bad, but at least he was not the one who denied the Lord three times before the cock crowed.'

Before she could say more, or quote directly from the Bible, Peter, looking somewhat embarrassed, backed away through the door and shut it in her face.

Elen stood there for a minute or two, sighing and tutting and muttering, 'Men!' But the bag was pressing on her back, so after a moment, she gave herself, and the bag, a little shake and knocked again.

The door opened promptly once more, and out came a man with a great file of papers under his arm. Elen realised that this must be Saint Paul.

Ellen stood there for a minute or two.

'Good afternoon, Saint Paul,' she began. 'You must be glad to be home after all those sea voyages. I have got my husband Jonah's soul here. He hasn't been that good, but he really wasn't all that bad either, so I would like to ask you to take him into High Eden.'

'Jonah?' murmured Paul, flicking through pages and running his finger down list after list. 'Let me see ... Oh ...' His expression changed. '*That* Jonah? Well, I'm afraid it can't be done. High Eden is not the place for him. He must go ... *elsewhere*.' This last word was said with a certain emphasis that made it more than clear exactly where he meant.

Elen's expression changed then, too, and if anyone from the market had been present, they would have quailed at this point. In stony tones, she said, 'My Jonah may have been a bit of a villain, but at least he never put saints in prison, nor "being exceedingly mad against them, did he persecute them even unto strange cities" ... Acts, Chapter 26, Verse 11.'

She could have gone on quoting the Bible, but Paul, his face red, turned round, went back into High Eden and slammed the door behind him, leaving Elen, and the bag, outside.

Now she cursed her own self for losing her temper and besting the saint for, while it had undoubtedly given her great satisfaction, it had left Jonah out in the cold. The bag on her back was so agitated that she could scarcely hold it, but she dared not put it down, for fear its contents would lose all hope. At last, with a great sigh, she knocked a third time.

And a third time, the door opened. Elen recognised the emerging figure at once. 'Lord Jesus,' she breathed, and made a little curtsey. 'It does my heart good to see your holy face. Blessed Jesus, I will tell you the truth, and nothing but the truth. Here on my back is the soul of my husband Jonah, who – next to me – was the most worthless of all your creatures. But I have hope that, in your goodness, you will give him leave to come into High Eden.'

Lord Jesus smiled kindly at Elen. 'I heard the promise you made to him, Elen, and I admire your grit. But really, you need to speak to Peter, my gatekeeper. Or to Paul, who keeps our paperwork in order.'

Elen's heart sank.

'And in truth,' said Lord Jesus, 'wasn't your Jonah more sinful than faithful?'

'So sinful,' wept Elen, unslinging the bag from her back and holding it out, 'That only you, in your infinite mercy, can open the door for him.'

'Believe me, Elen,' said Lord Jesus, gently, 'That is not in my hands.' He turned away slowly.

Elen's heart might have broken then if her mind had not been so quick. Jesus had spread his hands as he spoke, looking at them meaningfully. It made Elen look at her own hands, and the bag she held, and suddenly realise what her hands might do …

As Lord Jesus slowly, slowly, stepped through the wide-open door, and slowly, slowly, began to draw it closed behind him, she slipped the bag from her shoulder, held it tight in her two hands, and whirled it in through the door. Did Lord Jesus look back over his shoulder then, to wink at her? Surely not!

The door closed tight and the bells of High Eden pealed out to welcome Jonah home. Elen felt her heart as light as a feather, and she fair skipped back down the Long Welsh Tramping Road to her own little cottage, where the corgi was waiting for her, tail wagging, on the doorstep.

Elen and the corgi lived in that little cottage for many years more, until at last, it was Elen's time to walk the Long Welsh Tramping Road up to High Eden on her own account. And a warm welcome she had there.

16

SAVITRI AND SATYAVAN

Vrindavan is the forest. It is the place of exile, sanctuary, mystery, suffering and healing. There are stories of Lord Krishna as a child playing in the forest, where he and his family were exiled for many years. There are stories of Draupadi and her five husbands, the Pandava brothers, who were also exiled in the forest. They spent eleven years there.

The eldest Pandava brother, Yudhisthira, was the son of Dharma, god of right action. He was noble, brave and always told the truth. Sadly, he also had an uncontrollable gambling habit, and it was that which landed them all in exile in the forest.

One day, in the forest shade, Yudhisthira chatted to the sage, Narangar. 'Narangar, my friend. Life here would be unbearable were it not for Draupadi. She raises our spirits. She uplifts us and brings back the hope of light when all seems dark. It's only she who gets us going in the morning. Was there ever a woman who was as steadfast, bright and enlivening as Draupadi is?'

Narangar answered, 'Well, as you ask, and as it happens, yes there was. I'll tell you the story ...' And there, in the middle of the forest, he began the tale I'm about to tell you now.

Once, a king and a queen longed for a child. The sage told them that prayer was the key. They were both ascetics, so they fasted and prayed and meditated and one morning the king told the queen, 'Last night I had a dream.'

'Was there ever a woman as steadfast as Draupadi?'

She said, 'So did I.'

It turned out they had both dreamed of the god Savitr.

Now Savitr is an ancient and a subtle god. His quality is of the faint light in the sky before the sun rises. He's the child of the primaeval mother goddess. He is the possibility of creation, the possibility of protection, the force of the first movement towards change. He raises you up and he enlivens. He says, 'Things are dark. There will be light again. In the present darkness, look for the glow which is to come: put your attention there.'

The king asked, 'What did you dream?'

'I dreamed great Savitr appeared,' answered the queen. 'He had golden arms, golden eyes, golden hair, a golden chariot and broad beautiful open hands, and when he spoke it was eloquent and sweet. What did you dream?'

'I dreamed the same!'

'What did he say to you?' she asked.

'That we would have a daughter!'

'Yes. Me too!'

'Anything else?' he asked.

'Yes,' she replied. 'He said we need to go to bed together first.'

'Oh dear,' said the king. 'My dream didn't have that bit.'

'He said we would like it.'

'Really? Oh dear! I'm not sure.'

She said, 'It is required by the god.'

He said, 'Alright then.'

So, they followed the command of Savitr, and sure enough they were blessed with a beautiful daughter.

They called her Savitri, in honour of the god, and indeed, she seemed to have his qualities. Even while she was a baby, they found hope by stroking her chubby face and looking into her bright eyes.

When her father was engulfed in impossible decisions of affairs of state, he would pick her up and cuddle her. And suddenly there was the possibility of an answer. When her mother was trying to balance the budget and could see no way through the figures, she would spend a moment playing with little Savitri and when she returned to the work, there was the possibility of a different way of managing the books.

At first as a tiny child, then as a toddler, then as a schoolgirl, keeping company with Savitri helped you find an answer.

The time came when she wanted to marry, so they organised a Swayamvara. All the eligible young men came. She was a catch. She was a king's only child and beautiful, to boot.

But the Swayamvara wasn't a success. Though all the

young men who came to the Swayamvara found Savitri
fascinating and attractive, none seemed to want to take the
further step.

There were needy ones – they saw the capacity for protection in her and sought the shelter she offered. But at a glance
from her, they knew they had to learn to protect themselves.

There were bullies – they saw the light of the sun before it
rises and the trophy she would be and sought dominion over
her. But her glance told them, 'I am sovereign'.

There were thoughtful introverts – a glance from her eyes
was like a spotlight on their shortcomings and it sent them
straight off out of the door, determined to become better
men before they went to any more Swayamvaras.

Most young men saw her piercing gaze and were simply
intimidated, without quite knowing why. They left very
quickly too.

Her father said, 'Dear, this didn't work. I think you'll have
to find your own husband.'

So, she set off in search. She and her companions travelled through all the fashionable places in the city, then all
the unfashionable ones, then through other cities, then out-
lying farming trading areas, but the response was the same
wherever they went. They could find no eligible husband.
No young man could meet Savitri's gaze.

At last, they took an accidental track that led them
through the forest. Among the trees, an old woman and her
blind husband were brewing tea. Savitri respectfully asked
permission to join them. As they sat together, suddenly the
face of the old man brightened. He said, 'Wife, with my
sharp ears I hear our Satyavan is coming home.'

A young man was coming through the trees, dragging
a truck of logs. He was beautiful and strong. He bowed
when he saw Savitri. Though she looked at him, he did not
turn away. He recognised in her the light of the sun before

it rises. He was not intimidated. She saw he was not a lad who needed either her protection or her subservience. He was secure in his own integrity and honesty. Few words were spoken between them before she left, but they were both in agreement, and they both knew that she'd be back.

When she returned to the palace, the king and the queen were delighted with the news. The sage was very positive. He said, 'Yes, Satyavan is truly a fantastic match. I wonder that I didn't predict it. Let me check. Yes, he's marvellous!

'He's a prince, the son of a very good king and queen – the kingdom of the other side of the forest.

'Ah! I see it! Here is the problem. He has a very nasty uncle who has blinded the king, his brother, usurped the kingdom and exiled the whole royal family to the forest. Now Satyavan supports his parents by working as a woodcutter. But all this doesn't need to be a problem. He himself has an absolutely immaculate record. His name means "truth sayer". He always does what he knows is right. I see he's good looking and virile. She's made a really good choice and the marriage will be a success.

'There's just one thing. I wonder that I didn't see it before. He's only got a year to live, starting from a week tomorrow. Lord Yama, Lord of Death, who will come for us all, will come to fetch young Satyavan on that day. Neither he nor his family know of this.'

The king said to his daughter, 'I'm so sorry, my dear. Of course, you see that the match is out of the question.'

But Savitri did not see this at all. She paid no attention. She instructed the caterers. She sent out the wedding invitations.

The couple were married and went to live with his parents in the forest. There, they lived very happily together for a year.

Three days before the appointed death date, Savitri began fasting and meditating alone.

The family were puzzled. But she told no one what was about to take place.

On the predicted day, Savitri said, 'Dear Satyavan, it would please me to accompany you to your work today.'

'Of course. You know you can do as you wish. I'm delighted.'

They walked through the forest together till at last he said, 'Here it is. This is my place of work. Sit, sweetheart. Watch while I show you how good I am with an axe!'

She said, 'I will watch, while you do one of the many things you're good at.'

He walked a very little way off. She saw him speak to each tree and test it with a touch. She saw him walk from tree to tree, until he grasped his axe and began to raise it. But as he did, he staggered and fell on one knee. She rushed to his side.

He said, 'I feel so tired. My head aches. And look, I am sweating.'

She said, 'Lie down. Lay your head on my lap.'

And he did.

She stroked his head and began to chant, summoning all the power that she had been raising during the last three days of fasting and meditation. There, in the forest, she created a field of protection around herself and her beloved.

She heard a sound like the wind in the trees, but there was no wind. She sensed a movement at the edge of her vision. She knew she was in the presence of the servants of Lord Yama, Lord of Death. They were inhabiting the air around her circle of protection, attempting to enter. But she held firm.

The whispering stopped. There was a moment of respite when all was quiet. The beings were gone, but then came a clap of thunder and red and yellow storm clouds raged. Out of the clouds a figure was approaching. It was frightening – but she held firm.

She cried out the eloquent words she had prepared. 'I know you, Great Lord. Sweet Lord Yama. You are child of Dharma. You work tirelessly to do the will of Dharma. You work through the dark night. I welcome you and I honour you. All my praise to you, kind Lord!'

The storm died and there was Yama. He was tall and imposing and dressed in a red robe. He said, 'Daughter. I thank you for your eloquent words. Now stand aside.'

And she gave him the steady look that had intimidated so many young men, but it didn't work with the Lord of Death. So, she laid Satyavan gently down and rose. She said, 'I am pleased that my words of gratitude find favour with you. I ask for a gift.'

'What is it?'

'I ask for the life of my husband, Satyavan.'

She stroked his head and began to chant.

'That I will not give you. As you have so eloquently stated, it's my duty to do the work of Dharma, and it is my duty to take Satyavan's soul today.' He said nothing more, but held out his hand. A thread hung from it, with a little noose. The noose hovered above her husband. A small, almost imperceptible glow emerged from the mouth of Satyavan, and Yama caught the glow in the noose. Then Yama turned and strode away with the soul of Satyavan in the noose.

Savitri set off at a pace after the Lord of Death. She followed him to the edge of the forest.

There, he turned and said, 'You're following me.'

She said, 'Yes.'

He said, 'Why?'

She said, 'You've got my soul in your noose.'

He said, 'It isn't your soul. It's your husband's soul.'

And she said, 'That is an interesting idea.'

He said, 'What do you mean?'

She said, 'First, could I tell you just how much I like you? You are honest and forthright. No one tells you what to do. You just do what is right by your own judgement.'

He said, 'I can't help it. It's my nature.'

And she said, 'Yes, and you are true to it. I honour you, Yama, for Truth Telling and your forthright nature. Those are my husband's attributes too.'

He said, 'Thank you, but I will not give you back your husband.' And he turned and walked away, holding the little noose before him, and in it the glowing soul of Satyavan. And she followed.

She followed him through mountain paths and when they reached the desert, he turned and said, 'You're following me.'

She said, 'Yes.'

He said, 'Why?'

She said, 'You've got my soul in your noose.'

He said, 'It isn't your soul. It's your husband's soul.'

She said, 'It doesn't feel like that.'

He said, 'What do you mean?'

She said, 'I could tell you the story, but first, could I tell you just how much I like you? You are honest and forthright. No one tells you what to do. You just do it.'

He said, 'Yes, you said that before. And I told you that I can't help it. It's my nature.'

She said, 'Yes, and you are true to it. I honour you, Yama, for truth telling, and your forthright nature. You know Dharma, you know your duty, and what's more, you live your duty and you teach your duty to your followers and servants. They do as they are told, because you are kind and watchful and just and give each an equal judgement.

'Who would look after the forest and its inhabitants, but you?

'How would the forest revive but for you bringing down the old trees and the old stags? How would the old wheels turn, but for you?

'And who sings your praises?

'No one.

'How would we all be alive, great Lord Yama, but for your ministrations?'

He said, 'Stop.

'It's true. I have worked hard, aeon after aeon.

'It's true. Few welcome me.

'It's true. Your words are sweet, and I like them.

'But listen. You have to stop following me, and you have to stop talking.'

'One last thing, Lord Yama. You must know that if you take Satyavan's soul, you have to take mine as well. We are the same. It is the same thing.'

'No, dear daughter. That's not true. You and he are separate. And you will survive to live your own life. I will take him and I will not take you. But I like you and I'll give you a wish – except you can't ask for what is not permitted – you can't ask me to return the life of your beloved husband, Satyavan. You knew he was going to die.

'But such is the opening of my heart, through the eloquent words you've uttered, that I want to give you a gift.

'I, who am soothed by your words, will grant you a gift. I will grant whatever you wish: gold, riches – all these are within my gift, all. But I will not return of the life of your husband.'

She said, 'I wish that, within this year, my father-in-law will sit on the throne of his kingdom with his crown on his head, seeing me standing with my new-born baby, his grandchild, son of Satyavan, in my arms. That's my wish to you, Great and Beautiful Lord Yama. But how will this promised wish be fulfilled without my husband to give me my child? Hmm… I cannot think. How are you to keep your word?'

Yama put down the noose and looked at her. 'Your father-in-law on a throne? But his has been usurped.'

'Yes.'

'He sees you, but he is blind?'

'Yes.'

'You hold your new-born baby, son of Satyavan?'

'Yes.'

'You hold the grandchild, but the only son is dead?'

'Yes. Yes, oh great Lord of Truth. This is my wish. And you have promised to give it. Is it a great problem? Hmmm… Yes, I see it's difficult. How is it to be solved? Is there a way? I know you can surmount it because you have made me a promise, and your nature is honour and truth. So, you must bestow it.'

Lord Yama laughed. He said, 'This wish is a great wish, well thought-out and clever. I am delighted by it. Your words have been sweet and nourishing: I have enjoyed them, and I say: let your words be the creators of another possible world.

Let your words come into being. Dear child of Savitr, I give you what you want. I give you your father-in-law's sight and his kingdom. I give you your unborn child. I release your husband's soul.'

He flicked the noose in his hand, and the spark that was Satyavan's soul shot out and up and back through the forest. Savitri bowed deep in thanks to him. His form dissipated.

She ran and ran after the little spark, through the forest, till they came back to the body of Satyavan. She saw the glow disappear into her husband's mouth. He sat up.

'I release your husband's soul.'

When they got back to the hut, there was a big fuss going on because the old father could see again. Such wonder!

The day after that, a soldier came through the forest, saying the people were rising up against the bad brother and demanding that their good king come back. Such wonder!

And so, they all left the forest to return to their kingdom, and within the year she had a little one on her knee and her husband at her side. Such wonder!

Narangar finished telling his story.

'This is the story of Savitri,' he said. 'May we all leave the forest and come home with all our wishes fulfilled. Call on her name. Savitri is the beginning of the end of your suffering.'

Yudhisthira said, 'Thank you, Narangar. Thank you, Savitri. Thank you, Draupadi. We who have been exiled in the forest, we thank you. Like Savitri and Satyavan, let us all come to our true home again.'

WHAT MAKES A LIFE
WORTH LIVING?

The final two stories come from India and Ireland. Both explore what defines a life and makes it worth living.

With the Indian tale, we are back in the forest with *The Mahabharata*. Yudhisthira answers deep questions posed to him by an unknown spirit, who has the power of life and death. This is a test set by a strong patriarch about the parameters of a good life. The questions and answers are clear and prescriptive. They range from the specific to the universal.

In the Irish tale, it is St Patrick who attempts the patriarchal role, but with less success. Part of our version of the tale 'Oisin and St Patrick' draws on Lady Gregory's *Gods and Fighting Men*. Her translation from original sources was first published in 1904. She provides a detailed account of Oisin's prolonged dialogues with Patrick. Patrick is initially respectful towards the old pagan hero, but he becomes increasingly angry and rude as he attempts to convert him to Christianity.

The two exchange insults. Oisin calls Patrick, 'St Patrick of the crooked crozier', 'St Patrick of the closed mind',

'Patrick of the hindering heart'. For St Patrick, Oisin shifts from the 'man of good wit' to 'witless, grey, old man'.

And they spar, comparing their fathers: St Patrick's heavenly father God and Oisin's earthly one, Finn. Their dialogue covers the virtues of generosity, hospitality, honesty and forgiveness. They contrast church music and the sound of church bells with the music of nature and the voice of the poet.

Oisin's description of what he misses about the past emerges as much from frustration at his own ageing and his loss of an active role in community as it does from his sadness at the passing of the age and culture of the heroes. His description of the delights of Finn's house and the free life in nature, hunting, drinking and 'courting generous women', recalls Siduri's advice to Gilgamesh about what Gilgamesh is missing in his misguided search for immortality. In the Irish story, it is St Patrick who offers immortality. But Oisin is saying, 'My life will have no meaning without my place in the community that shaped me, so I choose not to live it.'

Although Oisin has clearly enjoyed his life to the full, his grief at losing that life is not mitigated by having valued the gifts of life. Lady Gregory's translation ends with a long howl of loss and grief, reminiscence and longing.

17

DEATH BY THE POOL

As you know, the five Pandava princes and their one wife Draupadi were exiled to the forest and spent many long years there, before they were restored to their proper princely state. One day, after twelve years of their wanderings, the brothers went hunting. They became very thirsty and, hearing the cry of a crane, knew water must be nearby.

Yudhisthira, son of Dharma, asked his brother Nakula to follow the call and fetch water. When Nakula did not return, Yudhisthira sent Sahadeva. When he did not return, Yudhisthira sent Arjuna. When he did not return, Yudhisthira sent Bhima.

When Bhima did not return, Yudhisthira went himself.

He followed the cry of the crane. He came to a shady pool, and there was the crane. There, too, were the bodies of his four brothers lying beside the pool, their mouths still wet from drinking the water of the pool.

Distraught, Yudhisthira went from body to body. He called their names and their good qualities and tried to rouse them. Then thirst took him to the water's edge. He cupped his hands and raised the water to his lips. But as he did so, he heard a stern voice speaking to him.

'Do not drink, prince. Before you drink you must face my questions. If you do not answer my questions, the water will be poison to you and you must face your death.'

Yudhisthira realised that each of his brothers had heard this voice and, in his thirst, each brother had dismissed it as merely the call of a crane; had ignored the imperative and died. But this was not the voice of a crane. This was the voice of a greater authority.

Sure enough, when he looked, he saw a shadow over the pool.

'I will answer any question you have with any little wisdom I have.'

The spirit of the pool began to speak.

'Good and well!'

And the spirit of the pool began to speak. 'Who makes the sun rise?'

Yudhisthira answered.

'Who keeps the sun company? Who causes the sun to set?

'How does one acquire intelligence?

'In what way are the Brahmins impious? What is the human attribute of the Brahmin? What is the divinity of the warrior? What is the human attribute of the warrior?'

Yudhisthira answered.

'What is of value to the farmer and the gardener?

'What is living death?

'What is faster than the wind? What is more numerous than grass?

'Who is the friend of the exile? Who is the friend of the sick?

'Who is the friend of the dying? What is the best guardian of happiness?'

And each one, Yudhisthira answered.

'What is the most valuable acquisition?'

'Knowledge.'

'What is the best thing to gain and maintain?'

'Health.'

'What is the highest duty in the world?'

'Do no harm.'

'Which friend will never let you down?'

'Friend Good will never let you down.'

'Which friend, if renounced, will change the world?'

'Pride. Renounce pride and the world will change.'

'What is the worst ignorance?'

'The ignorance that does not know its duty.'

'What is idleness?'

'Not discharging duty.'

'What is grief?'

'Ignorance.'

'Who is truly happy?'

'One who can cook in his own home and eat wholesome food. One who has no debt.'

'And Yudhisthira, answer this: What is most wonderful?'

'That every day, a myriad living entities die and depart to the abode of Yama. Yet, each human believes they are immortal and will live for ever. What can be more wonderful than this?'

'Drink,' said the spirit. 'Drink in safety. I grant you a drink because of your immaculate answers. And I give you a gift. I give you back the life of one of your brothers. Which one shall it be?'

Yudhisthira chose his half-brother, Nakula. He said, 'My mother Kunti will have me to comfort her. So poor Madri, mother of my half-brothers, will have Nakula to comfort her.'

'This last expression of kindness and duty has released all your brothers from their sleep, my dear son.'

Now Yudhisthira knew it was none other than his father, the god Dharma, with whom he had been speaking. He drank the water and it was refreshing and sweet. As he drank, all his brothers groaned and rose, as if from sleep.

18

OISIN AND ST PATRICK

In the beginning, the old gods were the ones that shaped the land of Ireland. Then it was their sons who blessed and cursed the land with the battles and the deaths and conflicts that happened there, and so the features of the land were named after those that died there.

In those days, they all lived at one and the same time on the borders of many worlds: the living and the dead; the fairy and the human; the elemental and the physical; the ascended and the grounded; the animal, the plant and the human. At that time, Finn Mac Cumhaill had a strong son born of the deer woman, Sadhbh, and so that son was named 'Little Deer', Oisin.

Oisin was called away from the company of his father and community by the true love of a fairy woman. He went out of this world and into the other and lived very happily there with her. But after a short while, he became homesick and longed for his own land, for his friends and for his father. His beloved gave him a white horse to carry him home and a warning, 'Do not step down from your saddle. Stay mounted at all times.'

When he returned home to Ireland, he found that while he had been away much had changed. For one thing, everything seemed smaller. Also, time seemed to move incredibly quickly. The people, too, were unbelievably small and very short-sighted, both literally and metaphorically.

A strong son born of the deer woman.

Oisin was a giant among pigmies, but he was soon to be a dying giant. He saw some people trying to drag a rock. Filled with pity for the little creatures, he leaned down from the saddle to help. But as he did, a strap snapped and he slipped out of the saddle and fell. As his foot touched this new earth, all his strength leached from him, his sight dimmed and he began to die.

Then a tiny little priest came scuttling up and squeaked, 'Oisin! I am St Patrick! I know who you are, and you must know that a new age has come! A new god has risen! I can baptise you in his ways, and if I do you will be admitted for ever into the glorious realm of heaven. Hooray!'

'What is the nature of this glorious realm?' Oisin asked the tiny priest.

'It is truly marvellous,' said St Patrick. 'Like your own father's feasting hall. But to get in, you have to be baptised.'

'And what's that?'

'Just a little good holy water to wash away your sins and everything that has gone before.'

'What? Wash away my past?'

'Yes,' said St Patrick. 'In order to get into heaven, you must change your ways and follow the rules of God.'

'And if I do as you say and I am admitted to this glorious realm, will I meet there the friends I long for – my father, Finn, and all the Fianna, and my mother, Sadhbh? Will I see my faithful hound?'

'Oh no,' squeaked little St Patrick. 'All pagans are excluded from the glorious realm. And no pets. In fact, I'm sorry to tell you that your father Finn is, in fact, in the other place – suffering the pains of hell.'

Oisin was upset. 'In that case, please intercede. Ask your father to free my father. Tell your father of Finn's many good virtues: he was always honest, never told a lie, was the greatest of hunters, the noblest of fighters. And as for generosity – he gave away gold to all.'

'No. It can't be done.'

'Why not?'

'Because of his disbelief in the true God.'

'Well,' said Oisin, 'I think my father had more generosity of spirit and more hospitality than does your father. Finn never forced a rule on anyone. Finn never refused a favour. Finn's door was never shut to any who asked entry. No one, weak or strong, rich or poor, was excluded. Patrick, free him from hell and allow him to enter God's feasting hall!'

'No, it can't be done.'

'Then the Fianna with their strength of arm will fight and free my father from his bonds.'

'No, it can't be done. God's power is irresistible. He doesn't fight.'

Oisin flew into a fury. 'And it's true your father's skill at fighting could never come near the skill of the Fianna. Where was he when we had to fight all those times?

'Where was he the time the two came from over the sea for the Queen of Lochlann of the Ships?

'Where was he when Dearg came?

'Why did the King of Heaven not protect them from the blows of the big man?

'It was not your father who saved the day, but my father, Finn.'

Now it was Patrick who was driven into a fury. He cried out, 'Stop your rambling! They are gone, and you are going!

'Leave your foolishness, witless, blinded, weak, old man.

'Your lack of sense is worse than your lack of sight.

'And if you had insight your desire would be for heaven.'

Oisin said quietly, 'I saw Finn last night. His skin lime-white; his hair golden; ready to work, gentle to women. His great, green vessels full of rough, sharp wine.

'I had a vision of Finn's house: Seven sides Finn's house had, and seven score shields on every side. Fifty fighting men he had about him, having woollen cloaks; ten bright drinking-cups in his hall; ten blue vessels, ten gold horns.

'It is a good household Finn had, without grudging, without lust, without vain boasting, without chattering, without any slur on any one of the Fianna.

'Finn never refused any man; he never put away anyone that came to his home.

'If the brown leaves falling in the woods were gold, if the white waves were silver, Finn would have given away the whole of it.

'I saw Finn last night.

'Then I heard the song of the blackbird. Oh blackbird! I never heard, on any height of the world, music that was sweeter than your voice – and you beside your nest. It's a pity not to listen to it, Patrick. You'd give up your lamentations and your clanking bells.

'The voice of the cuckoo on the Hill of Brambles, the early outcry of the hounds in the pleasant valley going over the strand of the Red Stones, the scream of the eagle on the edge of the wood.

'When Finn lived and the Fianna, it was sweet to them to be listening to the whistle of the blackbird; the voice of the bells would not have been sweet to them.

'Patrick of the true crozier, did you ever see, east or west, a greater hunt than that hunt of Finn and the Fianna? Oh, Patrick of the bells, that day was better to me than to be listening to your lamentations in the church.

'One time, Finn set us all to dragging stones for the building of a hall. And I would not. I said I would be under his sway no longer and I would obey him no more.

'"Oisin," says my father, "You yourself will be dragging a stone before your death comes to you."

'And he was right. I reached from the white horse to help to drag the stone, and here I lie.'

Patrick held up the holy water hopefully to Oisin, the dying giant. But Oisin shook his head. He said, 'And thanks very much for your kind help, dear little man, but why would I ever want to enter a realm that denies my father, Finn Mac Cumhaill, who was the descendant of many gods?

'Or that denies my mother, Sadhbh, who was the child of nature?

'Or that denies my family who are the animals, the trees and the rocks?'

And he turned his face from the holy water that was offered and, in the act, his form crumbled into dust. Unblessed and unshriven, he became a mound on the earth.

Patrick was very shocked. He was a kind man at heart, who truly believed he was right in keeping to his rule book.

They say that, after that, St Patrick felt he might perhaps have been inflexible in his approach. Some even say that, after that, Patrick and his followers learned the art of shapeshifting and running in nature with the deer. They went running over hills, sleeping in valleys and delighting in nature, as Oisin and his father, Finn, did in the years when they were living.

He became a mound on the earth.

Afterword

By June and Fiona

We have found solace and understanding through the process of shaping this book. These stories have spoken to us in profound ways. In writing our versions, we have tried to express the meanings we have discovered, and so we created the commentaries because we wanted to offer the reader a view into our process.

We have considered the important issue of cultural appropriation. We know that we have interfered with the cultural norms of some of these stories. However, we believe that telling an old story in a new way shows respect to the ideas held within it.

Our personal experience is that traditional stories give comfort in troubling circumstances, because their universal nature transcends time and cultures. In this way, they help us to feel less alone. They remind us that others have suffered, as we suffer now, and that, just as they survived, so may we. The stories offer us the comfort of our ancestors.

We invite you to explore these ideas of the ever after for yourself, and to retell, remake and work with these stories in your own way.

Like Jack in 'Death in a Nut', we all learn that there is a time to die, which cannot be avoided.

Like the Granddaughter who remembered her *Abuelo's* flute, we can all gain comfort in bereavement by caring for things that were important to our lost loved ones.

Like Oisin and Yudhisthira, we all try to answer: What defines a life? What makes it worth living?

As Gilgamesh learns, we cannot live happily ever after, but we can choose to live happily in the present moment.

And like Mary, we can ready ourselves to accept that our own death is part of the circle of life. Knowing life will not last forever adds to it both poignancy and sweetness.

Acknowledgements

We would like to thank our commissioning editor at The History Press, Nicola Guy, for supporting this unlikely project.

Our thanks to Alida Gersie for agreeing to write the Foreword, and for heroically reading our early drafts.

We also acknowledge all we have learnt from working, over many years, with our friends and mentors Tony Aylwin and Mary Medlicott. Although both have died, their wisdom and their stories live on.

We are grateful for practical help with this book from fellow storytellers Janet Dowling, Fran Hazelton, Maureen James and Anne Johnson. The debt we owe to other storytellers can only be partly acknowledged, for some of the stories have come to us through so many tellings that we do not know who to credit for first telling them to us.

Though we cannot identify the tellers of many of the stories we know, we offer grateful thanks to the following storytellers for introducing us to particular stories:

Tanya Batt, for 'Why Stones Live Forever'.

Abbi Patrix, for 'The Companion'.

Diane Wolkstein, for 'Inanna's Descent to the Underworld'.

Norma Torres, for 'Grandfather's Flute'.

Tamar Eluned Williams, for 'The Long Welsh Tramping Road'.

And finally, we are grateful to you, our readers, for sticking with us to explore this difficult but profoundly important subject through the medium of traditional tales. Thank you for your company. We hope you have found the journey worthwhile.

Society *for*
Storytelling

Since 1993, The Society for Storytelling has championed the ancient art of oral storytelling and its long and honourable history – not just as entertainment, but also in education, health, and inspiring and changing lives. Storytellers, enthusiasts and academics support and are supported by this registered charity to ensure the art is nurtured and developed throughout the UK.

Many activities of the Society are available to all, such as locating storytellers on the Society website, taking part in our annual National Storytelling Week at the start of every February, purchasing our quarterly magazine Storylines, or attending our Annual Gathering – a chance to revel in engaging performances, inspiring workshops, and the company of like-minded people.

You can also become a member of the Society to support the work we do. In return, you receive free access to Storylines, discounted tickets to the Annual Gathering and other storytelling events, the opportunity to join our mentorship scheme for new storytellers, and more. Among our great deals for members is a 30% discount off titles from The History Press.

For more information, including how to join, please visit

www.sfs.org.uk